Better Homes and Gardens.

THE PLEASURES OF

Cross-Stitch

First Edition. Fourth Printing, 1985.
Library of Congress Catalog Card Number: 83-61323
ISBN: 0-696-01080-1 (hard cover)
ISBN: 0-696-01082-8 (trade paperback)

BETTER HOMES AND GARDENS® BOOKS

Editor: Gerald M. Knox
Art Director: Ernest Shelton
Managing Editor: David A. Kirchner

Crafts Editor: Nancy Lindemeyer
Senior Crafts Books Editor: Joan Cravens
Associate Crafts Books Editors: Debra Felton,
    Laura Holtorf, Rebecca Jerdee, Sara Jane Treinen

Associate Art Directors: Linda Ford Vermie,
    Neoma Alt West, Randall Yontz
Copy and Production Editors: Marsha Jahns,
    Mary Helen Schiltz, Carl Voss, David A. Walsh
Assistant Art Directors: Harijs Priekulis,
    Tom Wegner
Senior Graphic Designers: Alisann Dixon,
    Lynda Haupert, Lyne Neymeyer
Graphic Designers: Mike Burns, Mike Eagleton,
    Deb Miner, Stan Sams, D. Greg Thompson,
    Darla Whipple

Vice President, Editorial Director: Doris Eby
Group Editorial Services Director: Duane L. Gregg

General Manager: Fred Stines
Director of Publishing: Robert B. Nelson
Vice President, Retail Marketing: Jamie Martin
Vice President, Direct Marketing: Arthur Heydendael

The Pleasures of Cross-Stitch
Crafts Editor: Laura Holtorf
Copy and Production Editor: David A. Walsh
Graphic Designer: Lynda Haupert
Electronic Text Processor: Donna Russell

Contents

The Pleasures of Cross-Stitch

A special joy goes hand in hand with the creation of beautiful cross-stitch embroideries. Whether you stitch for your own satisfaction or with a friend or family member in mind, each design is a warm, personal expression sure to be treasured for a lifetime.

Here are wonderful designs for you to enjoy cross-stitching—home accessories and fashion accents, gifts for special occasions, and suggestions for bazaar best sellers.

This first chapter is devoted to border patterns to use for a host of delightful designs, such as the sampler shown here. (How-to instructions begin on page 12.)

*B*order patterns are as versatile as your imagination—you can work them in rows (as on the diary or runner) or use them in single motifs to embellish small items (such as a sachet, hankie, or pincushion).

And because the motifs are small and quick to sew, border designs are perfect for bread-and-butter presents or other tokens of friendship, and easy to stitch up in batches for bazaars. On pages 16 and 17 you will find two dozen designs to stitch.

To get you started, here are seven creative ways to use just a few of the patterns. (You'll find more suggestions on the next four pages.)

The petite namesake necklace, *above right,* is sure to captivate a young lady. Letters spelling her name are worked over a single thread of white hardanger and then assembled into tiny pillow shapes. They are strung together with shiny pearl cotton flosses and wooden beads.

To make these for a profitable bazaar, stitch up a batch of letters, then assemble the desired name or initials upon request. (Be sure to sew them in a variety of colors and keep plenty of floss and beads on hand for stringing them together.)

The trio at right serves as a wonderful gift set worked with coordinating colors and motifs.

The appliqué on the diary is trimmed with tiny cross-stitched acorns and sewn with a lacy edging atop a softly padded book cover.

To complement the diary, cross-stitch a matching bookmark. It's embellished with a monogrammed perforated paper stitchery.

An elegant table runner, bordered with scrolling oak leaf motifs, completes the grouping.

Floral motifs and lacy edgings highlight the pincushion, scented sachet, and delicate linen handkerchief, *opposite.*

The pincushion is worked in a different manner than the other items because it is stitched in the Assisi style. This technique is worked by stitching the background area of the design using only one color of floss (pearl cotton floss is used here) and leaving the design itself unstitched.

Mr. and Mrs. D. Selby
6235 Franklin Ave.
Des Moines, Ia.

We're celebrating
Mom and Dad's 35th
wedding anniversary!
Won't You please join us
at home on Sunday,
May 20th at 3:00
in the afternoon?

Marsha
and Doug

Best Wishes
on
Your
Anniversary

8

STATIONERY AND CARDS

Colorful cross-stitch accents lend a personal, "designer" touch to the stationery designs, opposite.

These greetings are a delight to stitch and a joy to receive, too, because they show friends or family members that you think of them in a special way.

The invitation, gift tag, and note cards shown opposite are only a few of the many ways these designs can be used. For example, a recipe card trimmed with cross-stitches is a thoughtful gift for a wedding shower. Or stitch up a bundle for brief notes or letters. Use them for baby announcements, birthday greetings, place cards, and name tags—the possibilities are endless!

Colorful craft papers, perforated paper for stitchery, embroidery floss, and a few rolls of artist's graphic tape (available at art supply stores) are all the materials you'll need to assemble these delightful notes.

Each design is worked with two threads of embroidery floss over one space of perforated paper. The designs are then cut out, secured to craft paper, and bordered with strips of graphic artist's tape to give each a finished look.

Choose a small, uncomplicated design for quick-and-easy results. Stitch the design by the dozens, then package with matching envelopes to sell at bazaars, give as gifts, or use for personal correspondence.

For a unique bazaar item, the printed stationery, *above*, is a blue-ribbon winner.

Stitch a favorite cross-stitch design onto fabric, as shown *at right* in the photograph *above*. Then take the stitched fabric to a printer and voilà!—you've produced professional-looking stationery.

Because color printing often is costly, you should discuss prices and quantities with the printer before you begin.

You may find that it is more profitable to stitch and print the embroidered design using only one color, since each additional color increases the expense.

Also, because it costs almost as much to print 50 sheets of stationery as it does 200, be sure to shop wisely.

Beautiful packaging for your stationery is an important consideration when creating a bazaar best seller. Divide the printed stationery into groups of six, ten, or a dozen sheets.

Add color-coordinated envelopes, if desired, then tie them together with colorful ribbons.

*W*hatever your loving ties
to a baby may be—
mother, grandmother, or
simply a guardian angel—
celebrate the joyous arrival
with these gifts of stitchery,
handcrafted by you.

*The motifs that decorate
each of the items shown here
appear on pages 16-17. You can
create all of these cross-
stitched treasures using the
same motifs as pictured, or
select from any of the 24
patterns to design gifts with a
personal touch.*

The precious bib, shown at right
and below, is decorated with the
sweetest motifs in baby-soft pastels.
It's lined and padded with fluffy
quilt batting, then delicately quilt-
ed around the bordered edge.

Confectionery colors trim the delightful comforter, *right.* For any-
one inexperienced in the art of
counted cross-stitch, this is the perfect project because it's stitched
quickly and easily on pre-quilted
gingham with pearl cotton floss.

If the newborn is a little boy, you
might want to choose blue-and-
white gingham and a different border pattern. Then, trim the edges
with piping for a tailored effect.

Knitted garments for the little
one are especially endearing if you
add accents of embroidery.

The cardigan *at right, center,* fea-
tures a floral design stitched with
pearl cotton floss. Each cross-stitch
is worked over one knitted stitch.
(Be sure to select knitted items that
allow plenty of room for embellishment.)

The teddy bear, *opposite,* is oh-so
huggable because he is crafted from
head to toe entirely in cross-stitches. A complete pattern is given on
page 15 so you can make him exact-
ly as he appears here. However, the
bear's apparel is created with a
combination of border patterns, so
you can easily interchange any of

the cross-stitch patterns on pages
16-17 to make your own original design or create an entire family of
teddy bears—each with a completely different look and personality.

This charming toy is stitched
with bright pearl cotton floss on
Aida cloth to stand 10 inches tall.

For fun, why not change to a fin-
er, even-weave fabric, then work
the cross-stitches over one thread of
fabric to create a miniature bear?

Or, select a coarser fabric and
sew it up with jumbo stitches and
heavy yarn to make a life-size play-
mate for your child.

Patterns for projects in this chapter are given on pages 16-17. Use patterns noted in instructions, or substitute favorites. (See tips, page 75, to create your own designs.)

Home Sweet Home Sampler Magic

Sampler, pages 4-5, is 19x27 inches.

─────── MATERIALS ───────
- 23x31 inches of ecru Davosa cloth (or a suitable substitute)
- Embroidery floss

─────── INSTRUCTIONS ───────
Refer to special sections on pages 18-19, 32-33, and 54-55 for cross-stitch tips and techniques and for materials that are necessary for working counted cross-stitch projects.
- *To prepare the pattern:*
All patterns are on pages 16-17, except for the "Home Sweet Home," *right,* and the house, *opposite.* Pattern nos. 1, 2, 3, 7, 8, 9, 13, 17, and 19 were used on the sampler.

Chart sampler onto graph paper, starting in center of graph paper and center of border pattern.
- *To stitch the sampler:*
Work each stitch over two fabric threads using three floss strands.
- *To finish the sampler:*
Press and frame as desired. (See tips, page 53, for framing how-to.)

Monogrammed Necklace

─────── MATERIALS ───────
- Scraps of white hardanger
- Embroidery floss
- No. 5 pearl cotton floss
- Fleece
- Colored wooden beads

─────── INSTRUCTIONS ───────
- *To prepare the pattern:*
Use alphabet, pages 16-17, for necklace, page 6. Chart letters onto graph paper if desired.
- *To stitch the necklace:*
Use one strand of floss to work stitches over one thread of fabric.

- *To assemble the necklace:*
Draw a square around widest initial; use this square size for all initials. Cut fleece the same size.

Zigzag-stitch ¼ inch from edge of squares; cut out close to stitching. Cut backings the same size.

Sandwich fleece between square and backing. Turn under the seam allowance; stitch together. Quilt around the edges.

Using three separately threaded strands of pearl cotton floss, stitch through alternating squares and beads, knotting pearl cotton on either side of squares and beads. Allow length for necklace ties.

Diary Book Cover

─────── MATERIALS ───────
- Scrap of ecru hardanger
- Embroidery floss
- ¼-inch-wide ecru lace to trim stitchery
- Diary or book
- Print fabric to cover book
- Polyester quilt batting

─────── INSTRUCTIONS ───────
- *To prepare the pattern:*
Pattern nos. 3 and 6, pages 16-17, were used for the book cover, page 6. Chart the patterns onto graph paper (refer to photograph).
- *To stitch the appliqué:*
Use one strand of floss to work stitches over one thread of fabric.
- *To assemble the book cover:*
Draw rectangle the length of cover and the width of the circumference (from flap to flap) onto brown paper. Draw another rectangle the length and width of the *front* cover. Add ½ inch for seam allowances.

Cut two shapes for each rectangle from print fabric. Cut one long rectangle from batting.

Hem one long side on the smaller rectangles. For the flaps, place one hemmed rectangle atop end of one large rectangle right sides facing and matching raw edges; baste.

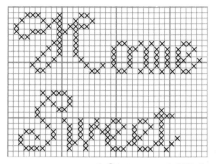

1 Square = 1 Stitch

Repeat, placing the remaining hemmed rectangle atop remaining end of large rectangle; baste.

Stack pieces as follows: batting; large rectangle with two hemmed rectangles at either side, faceup; and last large rectangle on top with wrong side faceup.

Stitch together, leaving opening for turning. Clip corners, turn, and press; stitch opening closed.

Press under raw edges of stitchery; trim with lace. Sew to book cover. Insert book into pocket flaps.

Stitched-on-Paper Bookmark

The stitchery is 2x4½ inches.

─────── MATERIALS ───────
- ⅛ yard of print fabric
- Perforated paper
- Embroidery floss

─────── INSTRUCTIONS ───────
- *To prepare the pattern:*
A portion of pattern No. 6, pages 16-17, was used for bookmark, page 6. Chart pattern onto graph paper. Chart an initial in the center.
- *To stitch the piece:*
Use two strands of floss to work stitches over one space of paper.
- *To assemble the bookmark:*
Trim stitchery to measure 2x4½ inches. Cut out two 2½x13½-inch strips from print fabric, adding ½ inch for seam allowances. Taper short ends into a point.

Stitch strips together, right sides facing, leaving an opening for turning. Turn, press, and stitch closed.

Quilt stitchery atop fabric strip, sewing through all layers.

Oak Leaf Table Runner

──── MATERIALS ────
- Ecru hardanger
- 1½-inch-wide ecru lace with edging for ribbon insert
- Olive green ribbon
- Embroidery floss

──── INSTRUCTIONS ────
- *To prepare the pattern:*
Use pattern No. 22 for runner, page 6. Transfer pattern to graph paper.
- *To stitch the runner:*
Use two strands of embroidery floss to work stitches over two threads of hardanger fabric. Stitch design to edge of runner.
- *To finish the runner:*
Trim runner to size, adding ½-inch seam allowances. Turn fabric under ¼ inch twice; hem. Thread lace with ribbon; sew to runner.

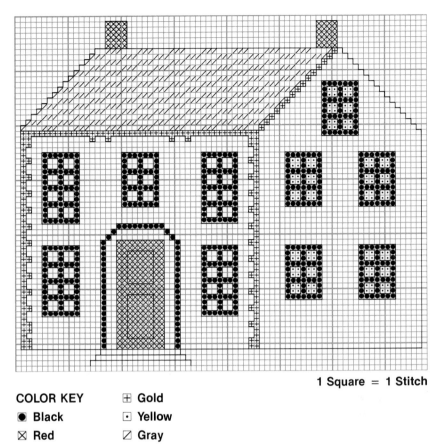

1 Square = 1 Stitch

COLOR KEY
- ◉ Black
- ⊠ Red
- ⊞ Gold
- ⊡ Yellow
- ⧄ Gray

Assisi-Stitched Floral Pincushion

Pincushion, page 7, is 3x4 inches.

──── MATERIALS ────
- Hardanger and backing fabric
- No. 3 pearl cotton floss
- ¼-inch-wide white lace
- Polyester fiberfill

──── INSTRUCTIONS ────
- *To prepare the pattern:*
Pattern No. 10 was used for the pincushion, page 7.
  To create an Assisi pattern, chart the background for the design onto graph paper; leave the design area unstitched. Add extra rows of cross-stitches around the design to create the pincushion shape.
- *To stitch the pincushion:*
Work the design with pearl cotton floss over three threads of fabric.
- *To assemble the pincushion:*
Zigzag-stitch ½ inch from edge of design; trim close to stitching. Cut fabric backing the same size.

Trim stitchery with lace. With right sides facing, sew the front to the back, leaving an opening for turning. Turn, stuff with fiberfill, and stitch opening closed.

Sweet-Scented Floral Sachet

Sachet, page 7, is 4 inches square.

──── MATERIALS ────
- 25-count even-weave rose fabric
- Backing fabric
- Embroidery floss in the desired colors
- Polyester fiberfill
- ½-inch-wide lace

──── INSTRUCTIONS ────
- *To prepare the pattern:*
Use pattern No. 19, page 17, for the sachet; make a mirror image of the border so the border encircles the floral design.

- *To stitch and assemble sachet:*
Follow the instructions for the pincushion, *above*, except stitch the *positive* design area.
  Use two strands of embroidery floss to work stitches over two threads of fabric; fill the sachet with potpourri.

Flower-and-Lace Handkerchief

Hankie, pages 6-7, is 11x11 inches.

──── MATERIALS ────
- 14-inch square of white linen
- Variegated embroidery floss
- 10-count waste canvas
- 1⅛ yards of 1-inch-wide lace

──── INSTRUCTIONS ────
- *To prepare the pattern:*
Pattern No. 15, page 16, was used to trim the handkerchief.

continued

Chart the pattern onto graph paper, if desired, using felt-tip marking pens.
• *To stitch the hankie:*
Position waste canvas *diagonally* in corner of linen, aligning canvas with fabric bias; baste in place. (See waste canvas tips, page 42.)
Use three strands of floss for working cross-stitches.
• *To finish the hankie:*
Cut hankie to measure 11x11 inches, adding ½ inch for seam allowance. Turn under ¼ inch twice and hem. Press; trim with lace.

Letter-Perfect Stationery, Cards, and Gift Tags

MATERIALS
• Perforated paper (available through Astor Place, Ltd., 239 Main Avenue, Sterling, NJ 07980)
• Embroidery floss in desired colors
• Craft paper (available in art stores)
• Graphic art tape (available in art stores)

INSTRUCTIONS
• *To prepare the patterns:*
Pattern nos. 2, 5, 8, 17, and 24 were used for the items on page 8. Transfer patterns onto graph paper using felt-tip pens.
• *To stitch a piece:*
Staple the perforated paper onto artist's stretcher strips, or work the piece in your hands.
Use two strands of floss for working stitches over one space of paper.
• *To assemble:*
Trim excess paper from stitchery.
Determine finished size of stationery, note card, or gift tag; cut out from craft paper.
Draw opening for stitchery on the *wrong* side of paper; cut out with a mat knife.
Tape stitchery in place. Border stitchery with graphic art tape.

Floral Stationery To Embroider and Print

MATERIALS
• White hardanger
• Embroidery floss

INSTRUCTIONS
• *To prepare the pattern:*
Determine size of stationery; draw outline onto graph paper.
Chart design in place (pattern No. 1 was used for stationery, page 9). Stitchery will be slightly smaller than pattern.
• *To stitch the piece:*
Use two strands of floss to work stitches over two threads of fabric.
• *To print and package stationery:*
Press stitchery; take to printer.
Tie printed stationery into bundles with ribbon. Purchase or make matching envelopes.

Gingham-and-Lace Baby Blanket

MATERIALS
• 42-inch squares *each* of pink gingham, quilt batting, and backing fabric
• No. 8 pearl cotton floss in pastel colors
• 2½-inch-wide white eyelet and 1½-inch-wide pink eyelet
• ¹⁄₁₆-inch-wide ribbon (quilt ties)

INSTRUCTIONS
• *To prepare the pattern:*
Use pattern No. 21 to trim blanket, page 10, or a favorite border design.
Determine finished size of gingham blanket. Count the number of squares on gingham fabric; chart blanket dimensions onto graph paper. Transfer pattern onto graph paper using felt-tip marking pens.
• *To stitch the blanket:*
With pearl cotton work one stitch in each square of the gingham.
• *To assemble the blanket:*
Baste batting to wrong side of blanket top. Stitch pink eyelet atop white eyelet; sew to blanket.
Sew top to backing, right sides facing, leaving an opening for turning. Turn, press, and stitch closed.

To tie quilt, thread needle with ribbon and take a stitch through all of the blanket layers; tie ribbon into a bow. Secure bows with tiny slip stitches.

Baby's Embroidered Floral Cardigan

MATERIALS
• Purchased baby cardigan
• No. 5 pearl cotton floss

INSTRUCTIONS
• *To prepare the pattern:*
Select a knitted garment that allows space for cross-stitching.
Count number of knitted stitches along the width and length of the area you wish to trim. Transfer dimensions onto graph paper.
Select a pattern and chart onto graph paper, adjusting it to fit if necessary. (Pattern No. 1 was used for cardigan, page 10.)
• *To prepare the materials:*
Select floss or yarn that is comparable to the weight of the yarn used for the garment.
Launder the garment and flosses first, so the dyes will not bleed.
• *To stitch the garment:*
Work one stitch over one knitted stitch. The cross-stitches will be slightly wider than they are tall since knitting stitches are not perfect squares.
Work the piece in your hands.
• *To finish the garment:*
To block, press on wrong side with a damp cloth and a warm iron.

A Newborn's Bluebird Bib

Bib, page 10, is 5½x6¼ inches.

MATERIALS
• 8x9 inches *each* of hardanger, backing fabric, and batting
• Embroidery floss in pastel colors
• ⅔ yard of ⅛-inch-wide lace
• 26 inches of bias tape

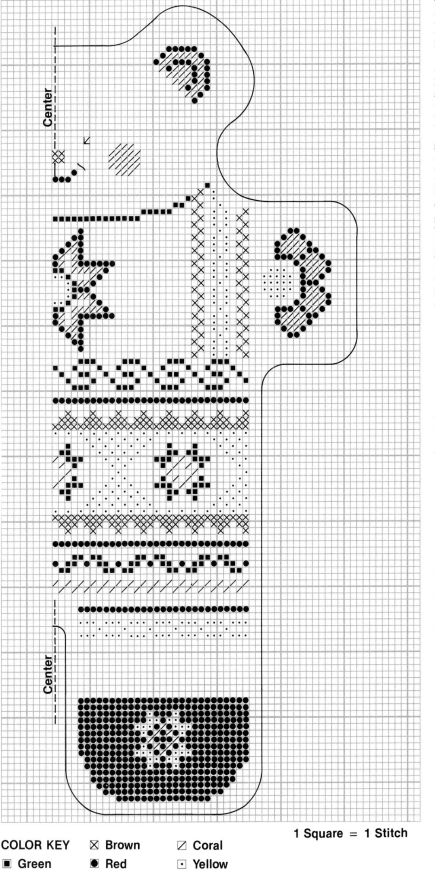

Center

Center

1 Square = 1 Stitch

COLOR KEY ⊠ Brown   ⧄ Coral
■ Green   ● Red   · Yellow

INSTRUCTIONS

• *To prepare the pattern:*
Pattern nos. 3, 8, and 13 were used for the bib.

Draw bib shape onto graph paper; chart motifs in place (refer to photograph). *Note:* Stitched bib will be slightly smaller than pattern.

• *To stitch the bib:*
Use two strands for working cross-stitches over two threads of fabric.

• *To assemble the bib:*
Draw neckline onto bib. Add ½-inch seam allowances around bib; cut out. Cut backing and fleece the same size. Border bib with lace; baste fleece to wrong side. With right sides facing, stitch front to back, leaving neckline open. Turn and press. Center bias tape along neckline. Stitch tape to neckline. Quilt inside border with pink floss.

Teddy-Bear Toy Dressed in Cross-Stitches

Bear, page 11, is 10 inches tall.

MATERIALS

· 14-inch square *each* of 11-count Aida cloth and calico (backing)
· No. 5 pearl cotton floss in colors listed under the color key
· 1 package of wide, red rickrack
· Polyester fiberfill

INSTRUCTIONS

• *To prepare the pattern:*
Chart diagram, *left,* onto graph paper. Make mirror image of pattern to complete.

• *To stitch the teddy bear:*
Work stitches over one square of Aida cloth with pearl cotton floss.

• *To assemble the teddy bear:*
Transfer bear outline onto fabric. (Outline is established by counting squares of graph paper and squares of fabric.) Zigzag-stitch ½ inch from outline; cut close to stitching.

Lay shape onto calico; cut out backing. Clip legs to separate.

Center rickrack atop bear outline; stitch. Press rickrack to inside.

With right sides facing, stitch front to back, leaving opening for turning. Clip seams, turn, press, and stuff. Stitch opening closed.

1 Square = 1 Stitch

STEP BY STEP TO CREATIVE EMBROIDERY

Counted cross-stitch is a delightful craft, and one that's easy to master. Learn just one basic stitch, and the technique is at your fingertips!

Some special materials and techniques will help you achieve picture-perfect stitchery every time. The information here will guide you through preparation of the pattern, selection and preparation of materials, and blocking of a finished piece. You will find tips on selecting threads, fabrics, needles, and hoops on pages 32-33. Instructions for working the traditional cross-stitch as well as creative variations of the stitch are on pages 54-55.

Also, throughout this book you will find tips on topics such as using waste canvas (page 42), framing (page 53), hemstitching (page 58), and creating your own designs (page 75).

By following the guidelines in this book, even beginners can turn out exquisite embroidery the very first time.

Start with a Pattern

Assembling pattern materials

Before you start, you will need to assemble the following materials: masking tape or transparent tape; graph paper; felt-tip marking pens or colored pencils; a ruler; pencils; and mat knife and scissors.
• *Graph paper*
Graph paper comes in many grid sizes, such as four-, ten-, and 14-squares to the inch. Because the patterns in this book are marked in increments of ten squares to the inch, a matching grid size is probably the easiest to use for charting out your pattern.

However, other factors may affect your choice of graph paper. For example, if the instructions direct you to stitch the piece over two fabric threads and you decide to stitch the project over four threads instead, you will get fewer stitches per inch. Consequently, you may wish to chart the pattern on graph paper with fewer squares to the inch to get a better approximation of the finished size.

Graph paper pads and sheets come in a variety of sizes as well, so select the size that best accommodates your design. If you have to piece sheets, carefully align the squares, then tape them together. (*Note:* Tape sheets on the *reverse* side if you are using felt-tip pens; pens will not color over tape. If you use colored pencils, use tape with a matte, not a glossy, finish; pencils will mark over the matte finish.)
• *Colored pencils and pens*
Use pencils or felt-tip pens in a variety of colors for charting the patterns. Felt-tip pens, although more costly, are probably a better choice. Ink from pens flows readily onto graph paper, and pens do not require sharpening. It takes more effort to color with pencils, and they need frequent sharpening.

Understanding a chart

To create beautiful stitchery, it is important to start with a complete and accurate pattern. Cross-stitch patterns are charted on grids with special symbols that represent the colors of thread used for embroidery. Symbols are noted in the color key accompanying each pattern.

Sometimes the patterns given in this book represent *only a portion* of the total design. The pattern shows either one quarter or one half of the entire design. The first step, then, is to chart out the *complete* design using the appropriate colors.

Charting the design

Look carefully at the pattern given in the book and locate the center of the *finished* pattern. Next find the center of the graph paper; with a ruler and a pencil, draw horizontal and vertical lines on the graph paper, marking the center of the height and the center of the width, respectively. Starting from this center point, begin marking crosses with pens or pencils. Chart the diagram as it appears in the book, then "flop" the pattern, making one or more mirror images of the printed chart on your graph paper pattern. (See the project instructions for specific directions.)

If you make an error when charting the pattern, simply eliminate the mistake using white typewriter correction fluid. If the error is over a large area, cut out the mistake with a mat knife and patch the hole with additional graph paper taped to the wrong side of the pattern. (Match the squares carefully.)

Choose the Materials

Selecting materials

Be careful to purchase adequate amounts of fabric and thread. If you are at all in doubt, a salesperson in the crafts store should be able to help you with selections.

Once you've purchased thread, jot down the color numbers, just in case you need additional amounts.

Testing for colorfastness

If you have selected deep-colored fabrics and threads, it is a good idea to check for colorfastness. Although most of the materials will not bleed, occasionally some do. For this reason it is worthwhile to take the necessary precautions. You can set dyes simply by dipping fabric or floss into a weak solution of salt and water, or vinegar and water.

When the fabric is dry, press carefully, then hem or tape the raw edges to prevent fraying as you embroider the piece.

Working with threads

Cut thread into lengths that are comfortable to work with; 18 inches is a good length. However, you may want to cut unusual flosses, such as rayons, silks, or metallics, into shorter lengths to make them easier to stitch with. Experiment with threads on scrap fabric before cutting lengths.

Knot the cut strands loosely together, and mark them with the color number, if desired.

Stitch the Design

Selecting a starting point

Determine where you will begin to stitch; this varies depending upon the design. Most often, the center is the best place. However, beginning in a corner is appropriate if you are certain of the finished size of your project. Mark the starting point with a tailor's tack or a water-erasable marking pen.

Be sure to allow extra fabric around the design for framing. You may wish to leave a border of plain fabric around the stitchery *before* framing, and you must allow excess fabric for stretching the stitchery around the cardboard or foam-core backing, too.

Mounting the fabric

Next, mount the fabric in a hoop, on stretcher strips, or in a frame, keeping the surface taut. For best results, maintain this tension until the embroidery is completed. See pages 32-33 for additional hoop and frame information.

Working the stitches

For an explanation of the stitch types and step-by-step directions for working them, see pages 54-55.

Using check points

Double-check the placement of the stitches periodically to prevent unnecessary ripping out later on. This is especially important when working with dark threads on light fabric, because the dark threads may leave a stain that would show if the threads were removed.

Examine your work periodically to make sure cross-stitches are *complete* stitches. And make certain the top stitch of the cross is worked in the same direction throughout.

If you are working a border pattern, stitch the basics of the border first to make sure your counting is accurate; add decorative portions to the border later.

Finish the Embroidery

Blocking the stitchery

Once you have completed the stitchery, remove the tape from the raw edges. Take a look at the back of your work, and clip the loose threads. Blocking the piece is the final step. Lay a thick cloth over your ironing board. Place stitchery right side down over the cloth. Dampen a pressing cloth and lay it atop the stitchery. Then press the piece using a moderately hot iron.

After blocking, the embroidery is ready for you to frame or assemble into the project of your choice.

Samplers and Sayings

Delightful combinations of border designs, alphabets, and individual motifs are the hallmarks of cross-stitched samplers and sayings. On the next several pages, you'll find those combinations in homey cross-stitched sentiments, a wedding sampler, and a romantic stitchery saying. Work the designs as they are shown, or combine elements from several to create uniquely personal projects for your home, family, and friends.

As the trio of gifts shown here demonstrates, you needn't confine your stitching to samplers. Using all or part of a single design, you can stitch this box top, mirror frame, and ruffled pillow.

For instructions, please turn the page.

'When This You See, Think Of Me' Pillow Top

The pillow, excluding the ruffle, measures 10 inches square.

MATERIALS

- 14-inch square *each* of white hardanger and backing fabric
- Embroidery floss (see color key)
- 1½ yards *each* of 2- and 3½-inch-wide white eyelet lace
- 1½ yards of 1-inch-wide self-pleated, pale blue satin ribbon
- Polyester fiberfill

INSTRUCTIONS

- *To prepare the patterns:*
Chart the diagram, *opposite,* onto graph paper.
- *To prepare the materials:*
Separate the floss and use two strands to work cross-stitches over two threads of fabric.
- *To stitch the pillow top:*
Locate center of the diagram and center of fabric. Place fabric, centered, in a hoop and begin stitching.
- *To assemble the pillow:*
Layer self-pleated blue ribbon atop eyelet laces, with widest eyelet on the bottom; baste together along top edge. Stitch edging around border of pillow top.

With right sides facing, stitch the backing to the pillow top, leaving an opening for turning. Turn, stuff, and stitch opening closed.

'When This You See, Think Of Me' Box Top

The box top is 7 inches square.

MATERIALS

- 9-inch square of 30-count lavender even-weave fabric
- Embroidery floss in colors listed under color key, or as desired
- ½ yard of blue print fabric (for box and lining)
- Heavy cardboard or foam core board (enough to line box)
- 1¼ yards of ½-inch-wide lace
- 20 inches of ribbon (box ties)
- Polyester batting

INSTRUCTIONS

- *To prepare the pattern:*
Eliminate the heart and outside border from the pillow pattern, *opposite,* to create the box top pattern; chart the pattern onto graph paper using felt-tip marking pens.
- *To prepare the materials:*
Separate the embroidery floss and use two strands for working cross-stitches over two threads of fabric.
- *To stitch the box top:*
Locate the center of the pattern and the center of the fabric.

Place the fabric, centered, in an embroidery hoop; begin stitching from the center outward.

Use the embroidery floss colors as noted under the color key, if desired, to stitch the box top.

Or stitch it as pictured, using the following colors of floss: With magenta, outline the flowers in the bouquet and stitch the saying and centers of tiny flowers surrounding the bouquet; with pink, fill the large flowers, stitch the ribbon, and work the tiny flowers on the border; work the stems and leaves with green; stitch the remainder of the border and tiny flowers surrounding the bouquet with gold metallic embroidery floss.

- *To assemble the box:*
From heavy cardboard or foam core board, cut two 7-inch squares (for the box top and bottom) and four 4¼x7-inch rectangles (for the sides of the box).

From polyester quilt batting, cut six 7-inch squares and twelve 4¼x7-inch rectangles.

From blue print fabric, cut one 10x30-inch strip (to cover the sides of the box) and three 8¼-inch squares (for the box top, bottom, and linings).

Glue batting to corresponding pieces of cardboard, placing two pieces on one side and one piece on the other side. The double layer sides should face outward when the box is assembled.

Note: Fabric measurements include ½ inch for seam allowances. Sew all of the pieces together, with the right sides facing.

For box top, trim stitchery to measure 8¼ inches square.

Gather lace; pin it ½ inch from raw edges. Stitch in place.

Stitch the box top to the lining along three sides; turn to the right side and press. Slip the cardboard into place.

For the sides, fold 10x30-inch strip in half; stitch together along long edge and one short edge. Turn and press. Insert one rectangle of cardboard; push to opposite end.

Using a zipper foot, machine-stitch 7¼ inches from the finished short edge to hold the cardboard piece in place. Repeat this procedure two more times.

Insert the last rectangle and turn under the fabric edges; stitch the opening closed.

To form sides, slip-stitch short edges together.

For the box bottom, sew the remaining fabric squares together; assemble as directed above for the box top. Stitch the sides to the bottom of the box.

To finish box, slip-stitch top to the box along one edge.

Cut ribbon in half and stitch one half to the top and one to the front side of the box; tie in a bow to close and trim ribbon.

'When This You See, Think Of Me' Mirror Frame

The mirror frame is 19x24 inches.

MATERIALS

- 23x28-inches *each* of 12-mesh mono needlepoint canvas, backing fabric, and interfacing
- Pink, peach, green, light and dark blue, and lavender $\frac{1}{16}$-inch-wide C. M. Offray ribbon
- Mirror, cut to finished size of framed piece
- Picture frame

INSTRUCTIONS

- *To prepare the pattern:*
Eliminate the saying and bouquet; chart the remainder of the pattern onto graph paper, subtracting two hearts from the width and adding two hearts to the length.

1 Square = 1 Stitch

• *To stitch the piece:*
Work the piece on a scroll-type frame, stretcher strips, or in your hands. Locate center of both canvas and pattern; count outward from center to begin stitching. With ribbon, work each cross-stitch over two threads of canvas. Be careful not to twist ribbon when stitching.

• *To assemble the mirror:*
Cut a rectangle in the center of the stitchery, allowing ½ inch for seam allowances. Cut lining and interfacing the same size. Baste interfacing to lining. With right sides facing, stitch pieces together around the mirror opening. Trim seams and clip corners; pull lining through to the back and press.

Trim the outer edges of mirror frame. Cut mirror to the size of stitchery. Place stitchery atop mirror; mat and frame as desired.

COLOR KEY
- ■ **Green**
- ◉ **Magenta**
- ◯ **Light Blue**
- ⊠ **Pink**
- · **Lavender**
- ⊞ **Gold Metallic**

A LOVING THOUGHT

*T*he sweet sentiments of
yesteryear are endearing
as ever. And the saying on the
sampler at right is a popular
favorite.
   *Yellow Dublin linen makes a
mellow background for the
stitchery. And a layer of
padding and delicate quilting
enhance the design.*
   *You can frame the stitchery
as shown here, or adapt it into
an album cover to give to a
special bride and groom.*

MATERIALS

- 15x18 inches *each* of yellow
  Dublin linen (24-count fabric) or
  a suitable substitute, quilt
  batting, and backing fabric
- Embroidery floss in colors listed
  under the color key

INSTRUCTIONS

*Refer to the special sections on pages
18-19, 32-33, and 54-55 for cross-
stitch tips and techniques and for
materials that are necessary for
working cross-stitch projects.*
   The finished size of the stitchery,
excluding the border of plain fabric, is 8½x12½ inches.
• *To prepare the pattern:*
Chart the complete pattern, *opposite*, if desired, onto graph paper using felt-tip marking pens.
• *To prepare the materials:*
Separate the embroidery floss and
use two strands for working cross-
stitches.
• *To stitch the piece:*
Locate the center of the graph-paper pattern and the center of the
fabric; begin stitching here, working outward from this point.
   Stitch each counted cross-stitch
over two threads of fabric.
• *To finish the piece:*
Sandwich the batting between the
backing fabric and the stitchery;
baste layers together.

With matching yellow thread,
quilt around the outside row of
cross-stitches and just inside the
dark green border.
   Work the quilting stitches over
two fabric threads and under two
fabric threads.
   Note: This step is optional, but it
gives a rich, padded appearance to
stitchery, and creates a lovely finish for needlework pictures.

Frame the picture as desired.
(See the tips on page 53 for stretching and framing instructions.)
   Or, use the stitchery to cover the
front of a picture album. (For how-
to instructions for making an album cover, see page 12.)

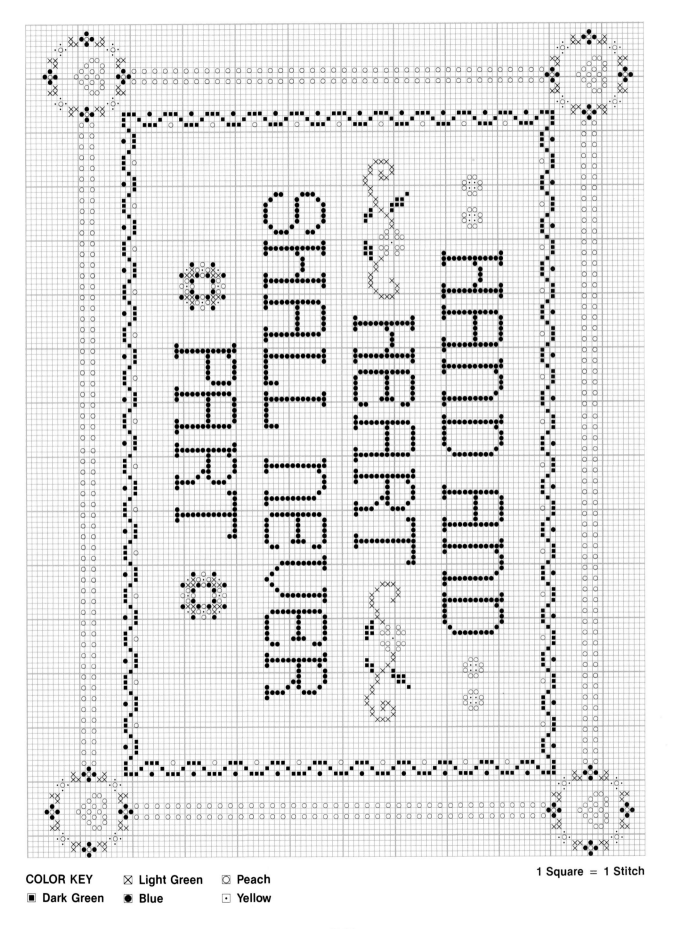

COLOR KEY ⊠ **Light Green** ⊙ **Peach**

■ **Dark Green** ● **Blue** ⊡ **Yellow**

1 Square = 1 Stitch

*T*his trio of samplers is a loving, heartfelt tribute to "home sweet home."

The traditional sentiments are bordered by sweet motifs that can be interchanged or rearranged with the sayings to make the samplers your own unique designs.

Each is worked with bright colors of floss on a background of white hardanger.

Make all three for a homey wall display or stitch one up for a housewarming gift to give to a special friend.

MATERIALS

· White hardanger in the following amounts: 13x13 inches for "Home Sweet Home"; 16x20 inches for "Be It Ever So Humble"; 12x13 inches for "Bless This Home"
· Embroidery floss in colors listed under the color key

INSTRUCTIONS

See pages 18-19, 32-33, and 54-55 for special cross-stitch tips and techniques, and for materials necessary for working all counted cross-stitch projects.

The approximate sampler sizes, unframed, are: "Home Sweet Home," 9x9 inches; "Be It Ever So Humble," 11½x15½ inches; "Bless This Home," 8x9 inches.

● *To prepare the patterns:*
Transfer diagrams, *at right* and on *pages 28 and 29,* onto graph paper using felt-tip marking pens.

Make mirror images of the diagrams (except for lettering) to complete the patterns.
● *To prepare the materials:*
Separate the embroidery floss and use two strands for working the cross-stitches.

● *To stitch the samplers:*
Locate the center of the pattern and the center of the fabric; begin stitching here.

Work the cross-stitches over two threads of hardanger fabric.

Stitch design from the center and work to the outer edges.
● *To finish the samplers:*
Block the finished embroideries by pressing them carefully with a damp press cloth and a warm iron.

Frame each sampler as desired. (See the tips on page 53 for framing ideas and instructions.)

1 Square = 1 Stitch

COLOR KEY

⊠	Navy	⊟	Gray
⊞	Red	·	Yellow
◪	Dark Blue	▧	Celery
◨	Light Blue	◧	Olive
■	Brown	◉	Coral
◕	Bright Pink	○	Pale Pink
◑	Rose	◪	Lavender

Center →

1 Square = 1 Stitch

28

COLOR KEY

- ☒ Navy
- ⊞ Red
- ◪ Dark Blue
- ◹ Light Blue
- ■ Brown
- ◉ Bright Pink
- ◑ Rose
- ⊟ Gray
- ⊡ Yellow
- ◿ Celery
- ◧ Olive
- ⊕ Coral
- ◎ Pale Pink
- ◪ Lavender

1 Square = 1 Stitch

Center

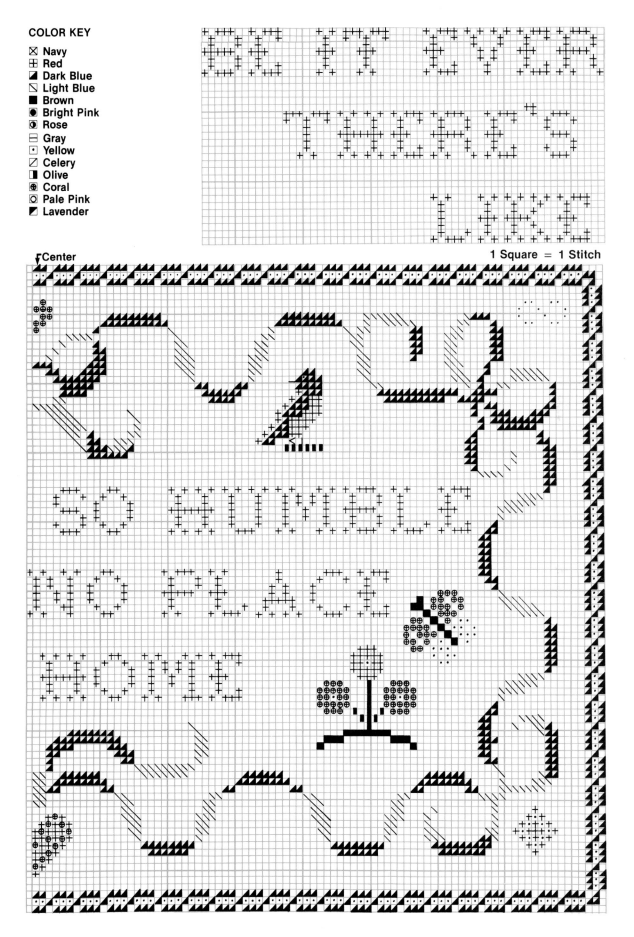

*T*his wedding sampler is a gift the bride and groom will treasure always.

Shimmers of metallic threads and a combination of cross-stitches, half cross-stitches, and backstitches add extra interest to this subtly colored stitchery.

Personalize the sampler with names, the date, and a saying chosen especially for the couple, using the alphabet, opposite.

MATERIALS

· 16x18-inch piece of ecru 25-count even-weave fabric
· Embroidery floss in colors listed under the color key

INSTRUCTIONS

The sampler is 9¼x10¾ inches.
• *To prepare the pattern:*
Chart the complete diagram, *opposite*, onto graph paper using felt-tip marking pens.

Chart names and sentiment inside center rectangle as desired.

• *To stitch the sampler:*
Use two strands of floss and one strand of gold metallic floss to work stitches over two fabric threads. Use one floss strand for outlining.

Locate center of design and fabric; begin stitching here.

With one strand of constrasting floss, outline all motifs, as noted on diagram, using backstitches.
• *To finish the sampler:*
Press sampler to block it; frame. (See the tips on page 53 for framing instructions.)

1 Square = 1 Stitch

COLOR KEY

▣ Dark Taupe	◪ Pale Taupe	⊟ Metallic Gold
⊠ Medium Taupe	● Rose	◩ Dark Flesh
⊞ Medium Light Taupe	◎ Light Pink	Ⅰ Light Flesh
	▲ Salmon	· White

HOOPS, NEEDLES AND OTHER SUPPLIES

*T*o help you create exquisite stitchery, we've assembled six pages of helpful cross-stitch information. On pages 18-19, you learned about the preparation of materials and patterns, and how to stitch and block a piece.

Here you will learn about the necessary tools. Although cross-stitching requires a minimum of supplies (fabric, thread, needle, and mounting frame), these selections are important ones. The information below will help you with these choices. (See pages 54-55 for specific cross-stitching instructions.)

Hoops and Frames

Selecting the right one

Finding a mounting frame that suits your stitching needs takes careful thought and consideration. Frames come in all sizes, shapes, and styles. You may want to consider several types before making a final selection.

• *Embroidery hoops*
One of the advantages of working with hoops is their portability. Hoops range in sizes from 3 to 23 inches in diameter. They are constructed of metal, wood, or plastic.

All types of hoops, whether metal, wooden, plastic, or spring tension, tend to leave marks on the fabric. To help prevent unnecessary soiling, follow these tips: Slip tissue or fabric between hoop and fabric to prevent soiling; avoid leaving fabric in a hoop for a long time; and cover the embroidered piece whenever you set it aside.

Spring-tension hoops hold fabric tautly, as do plastic hoops, which are designed with a lip on the lower hoop to grip the fabric (see examples opposite). Wooden and metal hoops will not hold fabric as tightly as either the plastic or spring-tension styles. If hoop tension is loose and you need a tighter fit, wrap the lower hoop with strips of fabric.

• *Artist's stretcher strips*
Stretcher strips, available at art supply stores, can be assembled in a wide variety of sizes. Stretch the fabric over the strips and tack it in place with a staple gun. Leave the fabric stretched over the strips until the piece is finished.

Using strips eliminates soiling created by hoop rims. The chief disadvantage of strips is that transporting them is cumbersome.

• *Scroll-type needlepoint frames*
Embroidery pieces can be mounted on scroll-type frames, but only if the piece calls for needlepoint canvas (see mirror frame, page 20). These frames have no tension control on the upper and lower portions of the fabric, and that is why they are suitable only for canvas. Scroll-type frames are awkward to transport, but they roll up, making them a better choice, in some instances, than stretcher strips.

• *Freestanding models*
Freestanding frames allow you to work with both hands but they come with one *standard* hoop size. Other disadvantages are that they are not portable and that you must sit up to them at all times. One freestanding model has an adjustable frame stand that comes with a movable arm. This style allows for greater flexibility and comfort than with other freestanding models.

Types of Needles

Distinguishing needle styles

Needles come in all shapes and sizes. They may be thick or thin, wide- or narrow-eyed, long or short, and sharp- or blunt-pointed. The type you select depends upon the threads and fabrics used.

• *Embroidery (or crewel) needles*
Embroidery needles, *opposite,* have a long eye for threading multiple plies of thread and a sharp point for stitching on closely woven fabrics. Use these, especially, if the project requires the use of waste canvas.

Embroidery (or crewel) needles are ideal when working with embroidery flosses, nos. 5 or 8 pearl cotton floss, metallic threads, thin cotton threads, or one ply of 3-ply wool yarn.

• *Chenille needles*
Chenille needles, *opposite,* have the same qualities as embroidery needles, but they are available only in the larger range of needle sizes. Longer eyes make them ideal for crewel embroidery and for cross-stitching with wool yarn or No. 8 pearl cotton floss.

• *Tapestry needles*
Tapestry needles, *opposite,* have the long eye characteristic of embroidery and chenille needles, but the end of the needle is blunt instead of pointed. Use tapestry needles to stitch on mono needlepoint canvas, perforated paper, and even-weave fabrics, because they will not catch or snag the materials.

Cross-Stitch Fabrics

Choosing even-weave fabrics

Counted cross-stitches may be worked on many types of fabrics. Even-weave fabrics are the obvious choice, but with the use of waste canvas, cross-stitches can be worked on a variety of closely woven fabrics, too (see *opposite*).

Chenille needle

Tapestry needle

Embroidery needle

Variegated floss

Embroidery floss

Pearl cotton floss

Ribbon

Three-ply wool yarn

Fabric strip

Vertical and horizontal threads of *even-weave fabrics* are the *same* thickness throughout the cloth. Fabrics come in many colors and thread counts, allowing great flexibility with the finished design size.

• *Hardanger cloth*
Hardanger is one of the more common fabrics used for counted thread work. The thread count is *always* 22 threads per inch.

• *Aida cloth*
Aida cloth is another commonly used fabric for cross-stitch. The cloth appears to be made of tiny squares. This is an excellent choice for beginners since squares define the area for working each stitch. Aida cloth comes in many sizes—6-count (referred to as Herta); 8-, 11-, and 14-count; and 18-count (or Ainring).

• *Mono needlepoint canvas*
Experiment with cross-stitches on mono needlepoint canvas, leaving the background unstitched. It is available in colors, and gives an interesting background effect.

Many other types of specialty even-weave fabrics are available to choose from. Just be careful to measure thread counts both horizontally and vertically before making a purchase. Some fabrics may vary by as little as one thread in one direction; this can throw off the stitch shape and the finished size.

Choosing other woven fabrics

Counted cross-stitches may be worked on fabrics other than even-weaves by using waste canvas (see tips, page 42).

Before purchasing a woven fabric, experiment with a threaded needle on a scrap of the cloth. This is especially important with unusual fabrics such as satins or taffetas because fabrics sometimes will "run," damaging the look of the finished piece. Also, some fabrics are so closely woven (for example, heavy denim) that it is difficult to pierce the fabric with a needle.

Gingham is a wonderful fabric for counted cross-stitches. Because of its obvious squares, it is perfect for beginners to work on.

If you use a fabric with lots of "give," back it with iron-on interfacing for stability.

Yarns and Threads

Selecting threads

• *Embroidery floss*
Six-strand floss is available in the widest range of colors. It is also available in variegated colors, which give embroidery a shaded look. (See page 41 for an example.)

Flosses are available in 100 percent cotton, rayon, or silk. (*Note:* When working with rayon flosses, run the strands across a damp paper towel for ease in stitching.)

Whether you use one or all six strands for stitching depends upon the fabric and number of threads each stitch is worked over.

• *Pearl cotton floss*
Pearl cotton is available in three sizes—nos. 3, 5, and 8. (No. 3 is thick; No. 8 is thin.) This floss has an obvious twist and a high sheen.

• *Wool yarn*
One strand of three-ply wool gives a rich look to cross-stitches. Wool can be worked over two threads of hardanger, although this gives stitches a thick appearance. Fabrics with fewer threads per inch are generally a better choice for using wool.

• *Miscellaneous threads*
The threads mentioned already are some of the more traditional cross-stitch materials, but there are other possibilities. Try working up a project with metallic threads (see page 20), ribbons (page 20), fabric strips (page 50), or string.

33

Pretty Florals to Embroider

Sweetly scented flowers, as beautiful as Mother Nature's own, blossom the year round when captured in needlework.

On the pages that follow you will discover a garden full of floral motifs for your cross-stitching pleasure, plus many suggestions that will help you make the most of each and every design.

The framed rose, opposite, is stitched with floss on perforated paper, but with a simple switch of materials you can create wonderful wearables, as well as decorations for your home.

For example, stitch the rose motif into a rag rug made from canvas and fabric strips, or cross-stitch the rose design with wool yarn onto a knitted sweater. (Please turn the page for instructions and a pattern to make the framed rose.)

Nelly Custis' Woodlawn Rose

*A*mericans can be proud of their rich heritage of cross-stitched embroideries.

Two such examples—from historic Woodlawn Plantation in Virginia—are the rose design, page 34, and the wreath-of-roses bookmark, at right.

Worked in delicately embroidered cross-stitches on perforated paper, both designs are the original handiwork of George Washington's adopted daughter, Nelly Custis Lewis.

MATERIALS
- 8x10-inch sheet of perforated paper (available through Astor Place, Ltd., 239 Main Avenue, Stirling, NJ 07980)
- Embroidery floss in colors listed under the color key
- Stretcher strips (optional)

INSTRUCTIONS
See pages 18-19, 32-33, and 54-55 for special cross-stitching tips and techniques and for materials necessary for working all counted cross-stitch projects.

The diameter of the rose motif, page 34, measures 6 inches.

• *To prepare the pattern:*
Transfer the complete pattern, *opposite above,* onto graph paper using felt-tip marking pens.

• *To prepare the materials:*
Staple the perforated paper onto stretcher strips for ease in stitching the piece. Or, work the stitchery in your hands.

• *To stitch the piece:*
Use two strands of floss to work cross-stitches over one square of the perforated paper.

The paper is fairly stable material. However, you should take some care when stitching the piece. Constant ripping and restitching of the threads may cause the paper to separate or tear.

• *To finish the piece:*
Mat or frame the finished stitchery as desired. (Before you begin, see the tips on framing, page 53.)

Nelly Custis' Wreath-of-Roses Bookmark

MATERIALS
- Perforated paper (available through Astor Place, Ltd., 239 Main Avenue, Stirling, NJ 07980)
- Embroidery floss in colors listed under the color key
- Two 3¼x4-inch strips of satin fabric
- Artist's stretcher strips (these are optional)

INSTRUCTIONS
• *To prepare the pattern:*
Transfer the pattern, *opposite below,* onto graph paper using felt-tip marking pens. Add an initial in the wreath center, and a sweet sentiment—such as "A rosy twine for thee" or "Friends forever"—above and below the wreath motif, if desired. Refer to commercial patterns for lettering.

• *To prepare materials and stitch the piece:*
Follow the instructions for the rose picture above.

• *To assemble the bookmark:*
Trim the perforated paper to measure 3¼x6 inches.

Sew the short ends of the perforated paper to the satin strips to make the bookmark.

1 Square = 1 Stitch

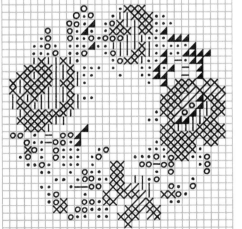

COLOR KEY

- ⊡ Dark Green
- ◎ Olive Green
- ⊟ Brown
- ◢ Off-White
- ⧄ Orange
- ⊠ Red
- Ⅱ Pink

COLOR KEY

- ⊡ Light Celery
- ◎ Celery
- ⊟ Olive
- ◣ Dark Olive
- ⊠ Dark Forest Green
- ● Rose
- ◹ Pink
- △ White
- Ⅱ Brown
- ⊞ Gold
- ◉ Dark Gold

GARLANDS OF ROSES

*F*rom past to present day,
the glorious rose has been
a symbol of love and beauty.
    The garlands that grace the
doily, at right, are elongated
versions of the same motifs
used on the paper picture
frame.

MATERIALS

For the doily

- 20-inch-square piece of ecru hardanger
- Embroidery floss in colors listed under the color key
- 1½ yards of ½-inch-wide lace

For the picture frame

- 9x12 inches of perforated paper
- Embroidery floss in colors listed under the color key
- ½ yard of narrow pink ribbon
- 8x10 inches of black mat board

INSTRUCTIONS

Refer to the special sections on pages 18-19, 32-33, and 54-55 for cross-stitching tips and techniques, and for materials that are necessary for working all cross-stitch projects.

For doily, use pattern, *opposite above.* Doily is 16 inches square.

• *To prepare the pattern:*
Transfer diagram onto graph paper using felt-tip marking pens. Make mirror image of area between the *dashed* line and line B, to left of line A; this is the basic motif (repeat three times for doily pattern). *Note:* Symbols to *right* of *dashed* line show placement for each repeat motif.

• *To stitch the doily:*
Separate the embroidery floss and use two strands for working cross-stitches over two threads of fabric.

Begin stitching along lacy pink border, starting beneath large rose, 2¼ inches from raw edge.

• *To finish the doily:*
Baste doily outline onto fabric. Zigzag-stitch ¾ inch from outline and trim close to stitching. Fold seam allowance under twice; hem. Trim doily with lace.

For frame, use pattern, *opposite below.* Stitchery is 6x8 inches.

• *To prepare the pattern:*
Transfer diagram to graph paper; this is lower right portion of design. Create lower left portion by charting area at right of line B to left of line A. Flop image to complete.

• *To prepare the materials:*
Staple paper to stretcher strips or work piece in your hands.

• *To stitch the picture frame:*
Use two strands of floss to work stitches over one space of paper.

Begin stitching lacy border be-neath large rose, starting 2¼ inches from edge of paper. Complete border, then stitch floral motifs.

• *To assemble the picture frame:*
Trim paper and mat board to desired size for framing.

Draw a rectangle slightly *smaller* than the photograph in center of both the design and mat board; cut out. Border the opening with running stitches (see diagram).

Cut ribbon into four strips; glue to underside of photo opening.

Glue picture to mat board; place stitchery on top. Frame as desired. (See tip box, page 53, for specific framing instructions.)

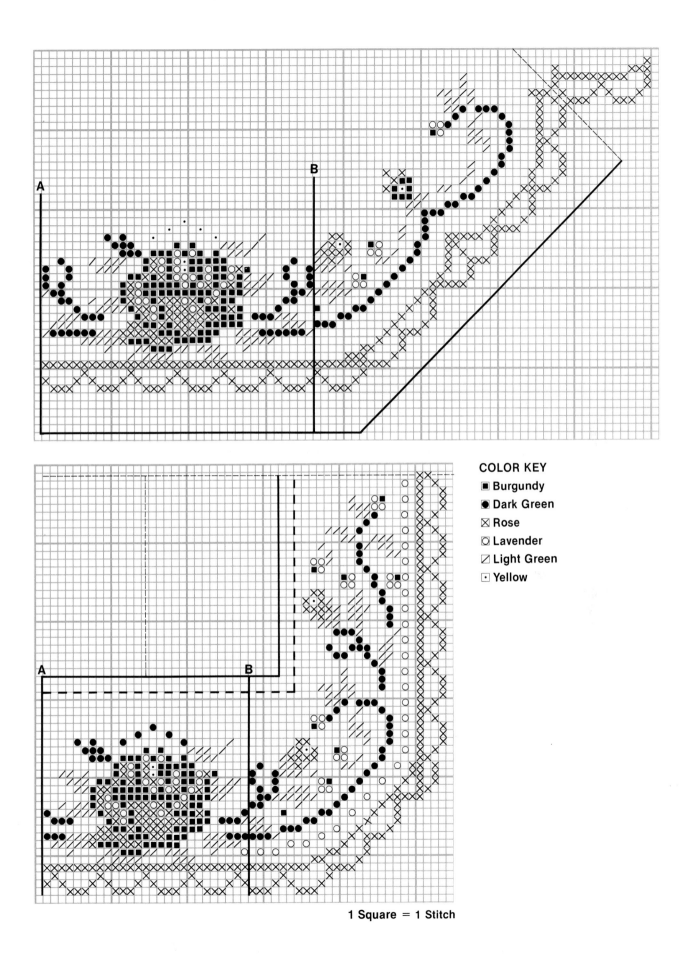

COLOR KEY
■ Burgundy
● Dark Green
⊠ Rose
◎ Lavender
◿ Light Green
⊡ Yellow

1 Square = 1 Stitch

39

S titched in summer's splashiest colors, this delightful rose-and-lattice pattern of yesteryear takes on a contemporary flavor that's simply irresistible!

Each of the stitcheries, opposite, is a variation on an antique table-runner pattern. By using the basic pattern and altering materials, you can create any of the needlecrafts shown here.

Variegated flosses lend a painterly quality to place mats and coordinating napkins. And waste canvas makes trimming a dress yoke, or any other garment, a breeze.

For yet another pattern variation using rug yarn, please turn to page 42.

Place Mats and Napkins

Refer to pages 18-19, 32-33, and 54-55 for cross-stitching tips and techniques, and for materials that are necessary for working counted cross-stitch projects.

The place mats measure 13x18 inches; the napkins are 14¾ inches square.

MATERIALS
· 16x21 inches of white hardanger for *each* place mat
· 18-inch square of white hardanger for *each* napkin
· Embroidery floss in colors listed under the color key

INSTRUCTIONS
• *To prepare the patterns:*
For place mats, chart the complete pattern, page 43, onto graph paper using felt-tip marking pens.

For napkins, border the rose motif, page 42, with a portion of the place mat design.

Refer to photograph and chart pattern as desired (one napkin side consists of 103 cross-stitches). Chart the rose motif into one corner of the napkin.

• *To prepare the materials:*
Separate the floss and use three strands for working stitches.

• *To stitch place mats and napkins:*
To begin stitching, start with the red border, 1½ inches from top and left edges. Work each cross-stitch over three threads of hardanger.

• *To finish place mats and napkins:*
Baste, then machine zigzag-stitch 1¼ inches from the outside edge of stitchery; trim close to stitching.

Turn a ¼-inch hem under twice; slip-stitch hem.

Cross-Stitched Dress Yoke

MATERIALS
· Commercial dress pattern with yoke inset
· Fabric and notions required for pattern
· Hardanger, broadcloth, and 10-count waste canvas (yardage amounts required for yoke)
· Embroidery floss in colors listed under the color key

INSTRUCTIONS
• *To prepare the pattern:*
Cut out commercial yoke pattern; transfer seam- and cutting lines onto graph paper (marked in increments of 10 squares to the inch).

One half of the place mat pattern is used to decorate the yoke. Locate the center of the width of both the graph-paper yoke pattern and the cross-stitch pattern. Chart design onto graph-paper pattern. Do not chart pattern in seam allowance. *Note:* Charted pattern may need minor adjustments to fit the yoke pattern. Move flowers closer to the neckline or farther away, and eliminate motifs, if necessary.

Fill empty yoke area with extra lattice pattern and tiny flowers.
• *To prepare the materials:*
Using dressmaker's carbon paper, transfer the seam and cutting lines of the graph-paper pattern onto white fabric; do not cut out.

Baste waste canvas to fabric. (See tip box, page 42, for canvas how-to.)
• *To stitch the yoke:*
Work design starting in center of neckline. Use three strands of floss for working cross-stitches. When stitching is complete, remove canvas; cut out yoke.
• *To assemble the dress:*
Follow pattern instructions.

Rug Yarn Chair Seat

MATERIALS
· Chair seat
· 7-mesh needlepoint canvas (to cover chair seat)
· Rug yarn in colors listed under the color key
· Polyester quilt batting
· Staple gun

INSTRUCTIONS
• *To prepare the pattern:*
Draw a grid on white paper to measure 3½ squares to the inch.

Trace outline of chair seat onto grid paper. Adapt the place mat pattern, page 43, to fit chair pattern. Fill center with latticework.
continued

- *To prepare materials:*
Mount canvas onto stretcher strips or a needlepoint frame.
- *To stitch the seat cover:*
Using rug yarn, work each cross-stitch over two threads of canvas.

Embroider floral, leaf, and lattice motifs; fill background with white cross-stitches, working extra rows around outside edge of design.
- *To finish and assemble chair:*
Block needlepoint; trim canvas.

Cut several layers of batting and a white lining to size of chair seat. Place batting atop chair seat and cover with lining; staple into place.

Center stitchery atop seat. Fold excess canvas around edge of seat; pull taut and staple to back side.

1 Square = 1 Stitch

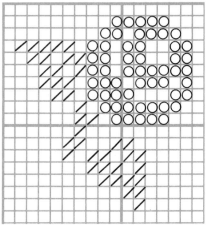

===TIPS===

How To Work with Waste Canvas

Waste canvas is a special fabric aid that enables an embroiderer to work counted cross-stitches atop fabrics other than even-weaves.

The finished appearance of the stitchery is identical to that of counted cross-stitch embroidery; however, a background fabric may be batiste, cotton, broadcloth, gabardine, poplin, wool, and a variety of other fabrics.

Working with waste canvas is easy and offers more options when choosing background fabrics.

MATERIALS
- Waste canvas to cover stitched area (available at craft stores)
- Needle and thread
- Background fabric

INSTRUCTIONS
Waste canvas comes in a variety of sizes ranging from 6 to 16 squares per linear inch. The canvas can be pieced, but it is wisest to purchase an amount that covers the entire area to be stitched. (Pieced strips often result in stitches that are not uniform in size or shape.)

Lay canvas atop fabric; make sure that the grid of canvas is even with the grain of the fabric and that a large square of canvas is *centered* over the fabric *center*. Pin and baste the canvas in place.

Begin stitching from the center.

To work the stitches, insert a threaded needle into the *smallest* squares of the canvas. (These are just large enough to accommodate a threaded needle.)

Be careful not to catch canvas when stitching, otherwise removing canvas threads is difficult and stitches will be pulled out of shape.

When the stitching is complete, moisten canvas; pull out horizontal threads, one at a time and in order. Then, pull vertical threads until canvas is completely removed.

COLOR KEY
■ Red Variegated
◎ Lavender Variegated
◩ Green Variegated
⦂ Yellow

Center

1 Square = 1 Stitch

43

*T*ake a pair of plain-Jane
curtains, add cross-
stitched borders of tulips, and
presto! You've changed a ho-
hum view into a country
delight!

*And because the motifs are
worked in a row, it's easy to
accommodate the tulip design
to fit windows of any size.*

*For a shaded effect, fill the
tulips with half cross-stitches
(see photograph, at right).*

———MATERIALS———
· Curtain fabric, broadcloth, and
  10-count waste canvas
  (yardages determined by
  curtain patterns, below)
· Embroidery floss (see color key)

———INSTRUCTIONS———
Use purchased curtains or make
your own. (If you make your own,
leave the bottom edges unfinished.)
Note: Subtract 5½ inches from the
depth of the valance and 4½ inches
from the depth of the curtains to
allow for border bands. The measurements do not include any seam
allowances.

● *To prepare the pattern:*
Transfer the pattern, *below,* onto
graph paper using felt-tip marking
pens. Chart a longer length of the
pattern, if desired. *Note:* This is the
pattern used to trim the valance.

For the curtain border pattern,
simply eliminate the row of motifs
just above the tulips.

● *To prepare the materials:*
Purchase broadcloth and lining
fabric for border bands.

Transfer the dimensions of the
bands onto fabric, adding ½ inch
for seam allowances. Do not cut out
the bands until all cross-stitching is
completed.

● *To stitch the bands:*
Locate the center of one fabric band
and the center of the waste canvas;
match centers and baste the waste
canvas to broadcloth. (See the tips,
page 42, for specific instructions.)

Use three strands of floss for
working cross-stitches.

Stitch cross-stitched bands; work
half cross-stitches in directions indicated on diagram. Cut out bands.

● *To assemble curtains:*
Sew appropriate bands to curtain
panels and valance; press. Hem, or
line the bands if desired.

1 Square = 1 Stitch

COLOR KEY ⊠ Olive Green
▣ Burgundy   ⊡ Bright Yellow

45

*H*erald the beauty of spring with the ever-fresh place mats, pictured at right.

Each place mat is trimmed with a glorious spray of pansies, strawberries, violets, or primroses, stitched with embroidery floss over two threads of hardanger fabric.

Create napkins to match, if you like, working each cross-stitch over one thread of fabric instead of two.

Also, because the motifs are so versatile, you'll find dozens of ways to use them, beginning with the suggestions below.

MATERIALS
- 15¼x20 inches of white hardanger for *each* place mat
- Embroidery floss in the colors listed under the color key

INSTRUCTIONS
Refer to the special sections on pages 18-19, 32-33, and 54-55 for cross-stitching tips and techniques, and for materials that are necessary for working cross-stitch projects.

Place mats are 11x15½ inches.

• *To prepare the patterns:*
Transfer the floral patterns, *opposite*, onto the lower left corner of the graph paper.

Chart a border row of lavender cross-stitches around each flower motif, leaving ten threads between the border row and the floral motif on *both* the left side and the bottom edge of each place mat.

Note: The border should measure 9½x14 inches when stitched.

• *To stitch the place mats:*
Using two strands of floss, work each stitch over two fabric threads.

Work the lavender border first, starting 3 inches from raw edges. *Note:* This allows ¾ inch for a plain border and 1¼ inches for the seam.

• *To finish place mats:*
Turn under seam allowance twice and slip-stitch a hem.

• *Creative ways with your designs:*
The designs shown throughout this book are a limitless source of inspiration to creative needleworkers.

You can use all of the motifs in many ways to make a variety of projects, simply by changing the number of motifs used, the stitch size, and the materials and threads used for the design. For example, you might use the floral motifs, *opposite*, in any of these ways:

Trim a dress yoke, pockets, apron bib, or napkins with a motif.

Stitch a design with wool yarn on a knitted garment (see page 51).

Frame a motif or stitch into a tiny pillow for gift giving.

Work stitches over one thread to create sachets, pincushions, box-top covers, and handkerchiefs.

Cross-stitch floral motifs in rows to trim a tablecloth, table runner, doilies, an apron, a skirt edge, or pillowcases and matching sheets. Combine rows of flowers to create a sampler. Or, stitch the rows with rug yarn or fabric strips on canvas (see page 50) to make a sturdy rug.

Center each motif inside a square or rectangle and set the shapes into a 15-inch square for a pillow top.

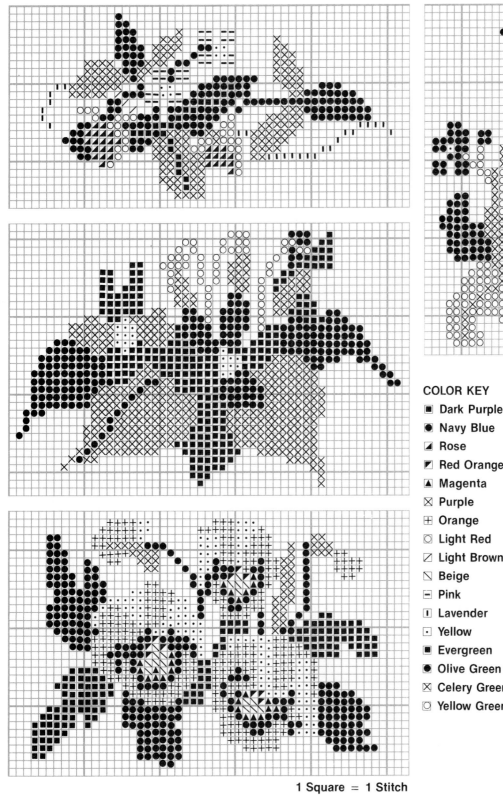

COLOR KEY

- ◼ Dark Purple
- ● Navy Blue
- ◣ Rose
- ◤ Red Orange
- ▲ Magenta
- ⊠ Purple
- ⊞ Orange
- ◎ Light Red
- ◪ Light Brown
- ◹ Beige
- ⊟ Pink
- Ⅰ Lavender
- ⊡ Yellow
- ◾ Evergreen
- ● Olive Green
- ⊠ Celery Green
- ◎ Yellow Green

1 Square = 1 Stitch

*P*ansies *blossom forever when you "plant" them on sprightly accessories for your home and wardrobe.*

The ring of posies, pictured opposite, is just the start. It is the basis for all the stitchery designs you'll find simply by turning the page.

Selected motifs from the pansy wreath adorn a knitted sweater, a decorative belt and bracelet, and even a rag rug cross-stitched with colorful strips of print fabrics.

With a touch of imagination (and a variety of materials), the possibilities are limitless!

MATERIALS

For the wreath picture
- ½ yard of white hardanger
- Embroidery floss in colors listed under the color key, page 52

For the sweater
- Purchased cotton knit sweater
- 3-ply Persian wool yarn in colors listed under the color key
- Straight pins

For the belt
- 5-inch-wide strip *each* of ecru hardanger, print fabric (lining), and interfacing, slightly shorter than measurement around waistline
- Embroidery floss in colors listed under the color key
- Two long bias strips to fit and tie around waistline

For the bracelet
- Scrap of ecru hardanger and backing fabric
- Embroidery floss in colors listed under the color key
- Ecru lace (edging)
- $\frac{1}{16}$-inch-wide ribbon in pansy colors (optional)
- 1-inch-wide pale-blue grosgrain ribbon to fit around wrist
- Two small snaps
- Polyester fiberfill
- Tissue paper and pencil

For the rug
- 27½x42 inches of No. 4-count rug canvas
- 44-inch-wide print fabrics in pansy colors (see rug instructions, page 53, for colors and amounts)
- 2 yards of 44-inch-wide white cotton fabric
- Rug binding

INSTRUCTIONS

Refer to the special sections on pages 18-19, 32-33, and 54-55 for cross-stitching tips and techniques, and for materials that are necessary for working cross-stitch projects.

For the wreath picture, see the diagram, page 52. The wreath diameter measures approximately 8½ inches.

• *To prepare the pattern:*
Transfer diagram onto graph paper using felt-tip marking pens.

Note: Purchase graph paper that is marked off in increments of 10 squares to the inch.

• *To prepare the materials:*
Locate center of hardanger and baste threads through this center point vertically and horizontally.

Then, baste vertical and horizontal threads every 20 threads of the hardanger fabric. Basted threads correspond to the graph paper lines and will help you count cross-stitches more accurately.

• *To stitch the wreath:*
Use two strands of floss to work cross-stitches and work each stitch over two threads of hardanger.

Use one strand of black floss for *outlining* leaves and flowers.

Begin stitching with any of the flower or leaf motifs. When the motifs are completed, outline each leaf, flower, and stem with back-stitches using black floss.

• *To finish the piece:*
Press the fabric carefully; mat and frame as desired. See tips, page 53, for framing instructions.

For the sweater, any of the motifs on the pattern, page 52, will work well as a decoration.

• *To prepare the pattern:*
Before charting pattern, make sure garment will accommodate the design. To do this, count the number of knitted stitches on the garment both vertically and horizontally.

Then, select the area of the pattern you wish to stitch; count the number of cross-stitches vertically and horizontally. *Note:* If design does not fit, eliminate or add motifs, such as leaves.

Chart the pattern onto graph paper using felt-tip marking pens.

• *To prepare the materials:*
Locate center of width on pattern and garment. Place a straight pin on the center stitch of the garment, *just below neckline.* Begin stitching from this center point.

• *To stitch the garment:*
Using 1 ply of the Persian wool, stitch a cross-stitch over one knitted stitch of the garment.

Following the chart, stitch the floral design on the garment. Work the cross-stitches with even tension and without a hoop to prevent the garment from stretching.

continued

49

Pearl cotton floss, embroidery floss, and a variety of other threads may be substituted for wool yarn, but it is important that the yarn or the thread thickness should equal the yarn weight of the sweater.

• *To finish the garment:*
Block the garment by pressing it with a damp cloth and a moderately hot iron.

For the belt, one size fits all because bias-strip ties make the belt adjustable.

The embroidered portion need not meet in the back.

• *To prepare the pattern:*
Select the pansy motif(s) of your choice from the wreath diagram on page 52.

Note: The pansy in the lower right corner of the wreath decorates the belt, *opposite.*

Transfer the motif(s) onto graph paper using felt-tip marking pens. Be careful to chart the first motif(s) in the *center* of the belt pattern.

Repeat motif(s) on either side of center motif(s) allowing uniform spacing between each repeat. (Five pansy motifs trim the belt.)

• *To prepare the materials:*
Separate the embroidery floss and use two strands for working cross-stitches over two threads of fabric.

• *To stitch the belt:*
Locate both the center of the fabric and pattern; begin stitching here.

• *To finish and assemble the belt:*
Press the stitchery carefully.

To assemble belt, sandwich interfacing between lining fabric and stitchery; pin and baste together.

Stitch bias tape to short sides of stitchery. Center strips of bias tape on long sides of stitchery, allowing approximately 18 inches on each end for ties; sew bias tape in place. Knot ends of ties.

For the bracelet, the medallion measures 2 inches in diameter.

• *To prepare the pattern:*
Any motifs on the diagram, page 52, will work for the bracelet. (We used two pansies centered on left side of wreath.)

Chart diagram onto graph paper. Use colors designated on diagram, or as desired.

• *To prepare the materials:*
Separate the embroidery floss and use one strand for stitching cross-stitches over one thread of fabric.

• *To stitch the bracelet:*
Locate the center of both the design and the fabric; begin stitching here.

Stitch motifs; then, outline with backstitches using one strand of black floss.

• *To finish and assemble bracelet:*
Lay tissue paper over the finished stitchery. Draw a circle onto tissue paper, around the pansies, using a protractor.

Transfer the circle pattern to stitched fabric using dressmaker's carbon. *Note:* This is the seam line.

Zigzag-stitch ⅜ inch from the seam line; trim close to stitching. Cut backing circle the same size. Cut grosgrain ribbon in half.

Sew lace to stitchery (right sides facing) atop basting thread. Sew front to back, leaving opening for turning. Turn, press, and stuff with fiberfill. Stitch opening closed.

continued

1 Square = 1 Stitch

COLOR KEY

■ Black	⊞ Bright Yellow	☐ White
▲ Dark Blue	⧄ Oatmeal	⊡ Light Yellow
◪ Burgundy	⛶ Medium Blue	▦ Evergreen
◉ Purple	⊟ Light Blue	⬢ Dark Olive Green
⊠ Brown	◎ Dark Peacock Blue	⊠ Light Olive Green
	◿ Medium Peacock Blue	⊟ Yellow Green

Turn under one raw edge on each grosgrain ribbon strip twice and hem. Slip-stitch the hemmed edge of each ribbon to opposite sides of the medallion.

Trim ribbon to fit around wrist, allowing ½-inch for seam allowances. Turn under a ¼-inch seam allowance twice and hem.

Sew snaps in place. Trim the medallion with ribbon bows, if desired.

For the rag rug, shown on page 50, the finished size is 25½x40 inches.

• *To prepare the pattern:*
Select the pansy motif(s) of your choice from the wreath pattern, *opposite.* (For our rug design, we used a cluster of three flowers from the bottom edge of wreath.)

• *To prepare the materials:*
Eighteen colors of printed fabrics, plus white, were used to stitch the rug. *Note:* The fabric colors differ somewhat from the colors suggested in the color key. Select colors as desired, or use those listed under the color key as a guide.

Wash the fabrics to remove sizing and to check for colorfastness.

Cut the fabric into 1-inch-wide strips that measure 44 inches long. *Note:* ½ yard of 44-inch-wide fabric yields 18 strips; each 44-inch strip of fabric yields approximately 14 *worked* cross-stitches on the canvas. For accurate yardages, count the number of stitches required for *each* color.

To prepare the strips, fold long raw edges to center of 1-inch-wide strip; fold in half again and press.

• *To stitch the rug:*
Work the rug in your hands for ease and flexibility.

Stitch each cross-stitch over two threads of canvas.

Stitch motifs, then fill in background and create the rectangular shape of the rug using white cross-stitches. Border with two rows of stitches worked using four shades of lavender print fabric.

• *To finish the rug:*
Turn raw edges under and baste to rug back. With right sides facing, sew binding to canvas edge, starting in center of one side, and keeping close to first row of stitches. Stitch binding to rug back; miter the corners.

How To Frame Your Stitchery

Whether your stitchery is a master work or the simplest of embroideries, its beauty depends upon the finishing touches. The way a stitchery is framed actually determines its success, and the tips that follow will help you turn out top-quality work, even the first time around!

─────── MATERIALS ───────
· Picture frame
· Polyester batting
· Backing material (foam core board, Upsom board, ¼-inch plywood, or cardboard)
· Brown paper, masking tape
· Mat knife, scissors
· Ruler, pencils
· Staple gun

─────── INSTRUCTIONS ───────
• *Measuring the stitchery:*
The first step is to determine the size of the backing the stitchery will stretch over. To do this, measure length and width of stitchery; add a seam allowance for a plain fabric border if you wish. *Note:* The frame will cover a portion of the stitchery on the front. Add to measurements for overlap.

Before determining the finished size, make an allowance for folding fabric around the backing; subtract ⅛ inch from width and length measurements. These final dimensions are measurements for cutting batting and backing material.

• *Purchasing the frame:*
Assembled frames come in many sizes and styles, and are available at framing shops and discount stores. Or, browse through antique shops, garage sales, and your attic for interesting frames. Unassembled frames are available, too, at discount or craft supply stores.

• *Preparing the materials:*
Draw measurement (as established above) onto backing material; cut out with a mat knife (except for plywood). Cut batting the same size. (Batting is optional, but it gives an attractive finish to the piece.)

Sew basting stitches along established measurements, and use as a guide for stretching the piece.

Locate the centers of the width and the length on all edges; snip fabric to mark these points. Mark corresponding points on backing.

• *Assembling the stitchery:*
Place batting atop backing; tape or staple into place.

Center the stitchery atop batting, matching notches on fabric with marked points on backing.

Pull excess fabric tautly over the edges of the backing and tape or staple to the back. (See diagram, *below,* and stretch the fabric following the numbers in sequence.)

Check often to make sure stitchery is stretched straight and even.

Once fabric is stretched from numbers 1 through 8, stretch areas *between* numbers, until every inch of fabric is pulled taut.

• *Framing:*
Secure stitchery into frame with framing tacks. Cover back with brown paper; attach wire to hang.

• *Framing with glass:*
If you use glass to frame embroidery, be sure to use spacers. Otherwise, glass will trap air inside, and over the years moisture will condense, causing fabric deterioration.

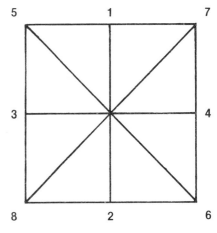

53

WORKING THE STITCHES

*O*n pages 18-19, you learned about purchasing materials, preparing patterns, and stitching and blocking a piece. On pages 32-33, you learned about the supplies.

Here you will find information regarding the basics of the cross-stitch—how to work a traditional cross-stitch (plus variations on the stitch), how to start and stop a stitch, and what the general appearance of a counted cross-stitch should be.

Traditional Cross-Stitch

Working a cross-stitch

To make a cross-stitch, pull a threaded needle from the wrong side of the fabric through a hole in the even-weave fabric. Carry the needle across four threads and up four threads and insert it in the upper right corner (see diagram, *opposite, left*).

The second stitch begins four threads below the upper right corner stitch; bring the needle up through the fabric at this point. Carry the needle across four threads and up four threads and insert it into the fabric at the upper left corner, finishing the stitch. *Note:* The number of threads a cross-stitch is worked over may vary from project to project. See project instructions for directions.

You also may embroider cross-stitches in the reverse direction; work with whichever method feels more comfortable to you. The important point to remember is that the stitches should be embroidered uniformly. That is, always work the top stitch in the *same direction.*

Using punch-and-poke method

The best technique to use for embroidering is the *punch-and-poke method* because it minimizes distortion of the stitches, allows for more even tension of the stitches, and lessens your chances of snagging fabric threads with the needle.

Each stitch of a cross-stitch is a two-step process. Insert the needle into the fabric and pull it through to the wrong side; then, insert the needle into fabric again and pull it through to the right side.

The punch-and-poke method is easiest when you work with *both* hands. If you are right-handed, keep your right hand above the piece and your left hand beneath it. (Reverse, if you are left-handed.) It may be awkward at first, but with a little patience and practice, you'll find stitching easier and faster.

Maintaining even tension

When embroidering, keep the stitch tension uniform. If threads are pulled too taut, the fabric and stitches become distorted. If the threads are too loose, you will lose the shape of the stitch.

Stitching correct proportions

The choice of thread depends entirely upon the fabric selected. Take care to purchase threads that will give the stitch its proper proportions on the fabric you have selected. *Note:* If you use threads with several plies, such as yarn or floss, it is necessary to establish the correct number of plies to use. Experiment with the thread and fabric you wish to use before you purchase large quantities of materials. Or discuss these selections with the salespeople at your local needlecrafts store; they should be able to help you with selections.

In the illustrations, *opposite, left,* the cross-stitches are worked over four threads of hardanger using cotton embroidery floss. The first example shows stitches embroidered with three strands of the floss; the cross-stitches are too skinny and lightweight when worked over four threads of this fabric.

The second example uses 12 strands; the stitches are too bulky when worked over four threads. (Using too many strands often creates problems when stitching; it becomes increasingly difficult to pull the floss through spaces in even-weave fabrics.)

The third example illustrates the proper weight for the stitch size. Six strands have been used here.

Beginning and ending a stitch

The best way to begin a cross-stitch is by using a waste knot. It is a temporary knot and will be clipped when no longer necessary. To begin, knot the end of a threaded needle. Insert the needle into the right side of the fabric, about 4 inches away from placement of the first cross-stitch. Bring the needle up through the fabric and work the first series of cross-stitches. Stitch until thread is used up or until the area using this color is complete.

To finish the thread, slip the threaded needle under the previously stitched threads on the wrong side of the fabric for 1 to 1½ inches. (You may wish to weave the thread back and forth a few times.) Clip the thread.

Turn the piece to the right side and clip the knot. Rethread the needle with the excess floss, push the needle through to the wrong side of the stitchery, and finish the thread off as directed above.

Carrying threads

If you are working with areas that use a variety of thread colors (for example, a multicolored bouquet of tiny flowers), you may not wish to begin and end your thread every time you stitch a flower or an individual leaf. In these instances, carry thread across the back of the fabric, but, to secure the thread, slip the threaded needle under previously stitched crosses.

If you carry the threads *loosely* to another area, the piece can easily become distorted: If the tension is too tight, the fabric tends to bunch up; if the tension is too loose, the back becomes messy and threads may tangle and twist.

Making the wrong side 'right'

Although the appearance of the back of a stitchery may not seem as important as the front, many embroiderers are concerned about the neatness and uniformity of the stitches on the underside of their work. The direction of the stitches on the reverse side should be vertical *as often as possible.* (An occasional horizontal stitch is unavoidable.) Experiment on scrap fabric until this is comfortable.

Cross-Stitch Variations

Altering the basic stitch

Many types of cross-stitches are variations on the basic stitch. By changing the length and direction of the stitches and by crossing them as many times as you like, you can create an endless number of cross-stitch patterns. Displayed *at far right* are just a few of the imaginative possibilities; a description of the stitches follows.

• *Traditional cross-stitch:* Worked with variegated floss, this is the most commonly used cross-stitch. (See stitch instructions, *opposite.*)

• *Half cross-stitch:* Work only the first step of the traditional stitch (in either direction) for a half cross-stitch. The sample *at upper right* is worked with pearl cotton floss.

Working a cross-stitch

3 strands

12 strands

6 strands

• *Double cross-stitch:* Work a traditional cross-stitch, then work an upright cross-stitch atop the first stitch. The steps may be reversed, *above right.*

• *Three-quarter cross-stitch:* Work a half cross-stitch. Then stitch *half* of the "arm" of the second stitch in any direction. The example shows four stitch variations, worked with different colors of floss.

• *Italian stitch:* Stitch a traditional cross-stitch, then surround the cross with straight stitches.

• *Rice stitch:* Work a traditional cross-stitch. Then cross the arms of the cross-stitch with small half cross-stitches. (Half crosses shown are worked with metallic thread.)

• *Herringbone stitch:* This is a variation of the long-armed cross-stitch. Each arm of the stitch is identical in length; however, the arms do not cross in the center of the stitch.

• *Long-armed cross-stitch:* Work one arm of the cross-stitch longer than the other. The short arm of the stitch may cross the long arm at any place (see example).

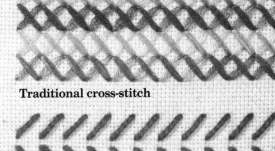

Traditional cross-stitch

Half cross-stitch

Double cross-stitch

Three-quarter cross-stitch

Italian cross-stitch

Rice cross-stitch

Herringbone cross-stitch

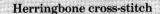

Long-armed cross-stitch

55

Very Special Gifts

A handmade piece of needlework is a treasured token of love and friendship because it takes special care to stitch a gift that is "just right" for the lucky recipient. On the pages that follow, you will find a floral-embroidered apron, pillows, bed linens, and an exquisite picture frame—befitting ideas for almost every gift-giving occasion.

For example, the quail designs, *opposite,* are simple to stitch but appropriate gifts for a father, grand-father, bird fancier, or sportsman.

For instructions for making the picture, tie, and book cover, see page 58.

Quail
Album Cover

MATERIALS

· Plaid wool fabric for cover
· Scrap of beige 13-count even-weave fabric
· Embroidery floss in the desired colors
· Black piping (to trim stitchery)
· Polyester quilt batting

INSTRUCTIONS

· *To prepare the pattern:*
Transfer pattern for large quail, *at right,* onto graph paper using felt-tip marking pens. Vary the colors on the quails; arrange as desired.

· *To stitch the quails:*
Use two strands of embroidery floss to work the cross-stitches over one thread of the fabric. Work straight stitches for grass with light and dark green floss.

· *To assemble album cover:*
See instructions for diary book cover, page 12.

Trim stitchery, adding ½-inch seam allowances; trim with piping. Press under seam allowance; sew to cover. Insert book into pocket flaps.

Quail Picture
and Necktie

Picture, unframed, is 5x20 inches.

MATERIALS

For picture
· 13-count ecru even-weave fabric
· Embroidery floss
For necktie
· Purchased tie
· Embroidery floss
· 10-count waste canvas

INSTRUCTIONS

For picture—
· *To prepare the pattern:*
Using alphabet, pages 16-17, chart out DAD or name desired.

Chart one large quail and several small quail, *above right,* onto graph paper, and arrange as desired. Add grass around each quail.

· *To stitch the piece:*
Use six strands of floss and work stitches over two fabric threads.

For a Fine Finish— Hemstitching

Hemstitching adds a nice decorative touch to delicate embroidery and provides a framework for a fringe on finely woven fabrics.

To work this lovely hem, make sure the raw edge of the embroidery is perfectly straight by removing a thread and cutting the fabric along the channel that is created. Fold under the raw edges, turn up the hem, and baste.

Turn cloth so wrong side faces you and carefully snip two to four threads parallel to hem, directly above upper fold of hem.

To work hemstitching, follow diagram *(below left).* Slip the knotted thread end under the fold and bring thread through the hem two threads below drawn area. Insert the needle three or four threads to the right and in drawn area. Go under three or four threads; bring it up again in the drawn area. Cross over three or four threads; reinsert the needle, slipping it under the fold and bringing it out again two threads below the drawn area. Pull the thread snug; repeat.

A second row of stitches may be added to top of drawn area, wrapping same threads as before to create a ladder *(below, center).* Or wrap alternate ones *(below, right).*

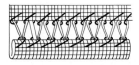

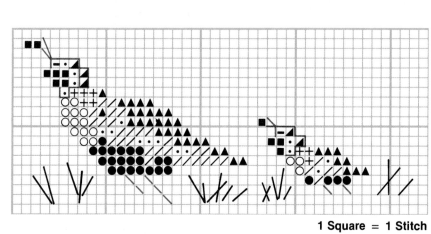

1 Square = 1 Stitch

COLOR KEY

◼ Black	◣ Rust	⬤ Dark Gold	Red lines
⊡ White	▲ Dark Taupe	⊟ Light Gold	indicate black
⊞ Gray	⁄ Light Taupe	◯ Blue-Gray	backstitches

· *To finish the piece:*
Press the stitchery and frame as desired. (See the tips on page 53 for framing instructions.)
For necktie—
· *To prepare the pattern:*
Chart small quail pattern, *above,* onto graph paper.

· *To stitch the necktie:*
Remove the stitching on the back of the tie. Baste waste canvas to front. (See waste canvas tips, page 42.)

Use two strands of embroidery floss to work cross-stitches.

· *To finish the necktie:*
Restitch back seam, and press.

58

A Stitchery Sampler on
HANDKERCHIEF PILLOWS

*I*n days past, a young girl's first attempt at embroidery usually was a long, narrow sampler consisting of basic stitches. This piece functioned as a learning tool and was rolled up and consulted whenever necessary.

The handkerchief pillows at right are learning samplers, too. Each is trimmed with cross-stitches and stitch variations. They function in much the same manner as did the narrow samplers of long ago, and serve a decorative purpose as well!

─────MATERIALS─────
· Two 18- or 19-inch plaid men's handkerchiefs (or other suitable plaid fabrics) *for each pillow*
· 12-inch pillow forms (or polyester fiberfill)
· 3-ply wool yarn in a variety of colors

─────INSTRUCTIONS─────
Refer to pages 18-19, 32-33, and 54-55 for cross-stitching tips and techniques, and for materials that are necessary for working all counted cross-stitch projects.

● *To prepare the patterns:*
The pillows shown here are samplers of traditional cross-stitches and cross-stitch variations. (See pages 54-55 for stitch identification and how-to instructions.)

Since the designs for each pillow depend upon the plaid fabrics chosen, no specific patterns are given. Each design shown above is worked in a free-form manner. However, you may chart out a pattern, if you wish, onto graph paper using felt-tip marking pens. To do this, onto brown paper draw a grid identical to the grid of the fabric chosen; mark stitches onto grid.

● *To prepare the materials:*
Separate the 3-ply wool and use 1 strand for stitching cross-stitches.

Center the handkerchief in an embroidery hoop.
● *To stitch the pillows:*
Start in the center of the handkerchief or fabric and work rows of pattern to the outer edges.

Experiment with as many variations of the traditional cross-stitch as desired. Vary the colors and the sizes of the stitches for additional interest.

Work the cross-stitches on one handkerchief (pillow front).
● *To assemble the pillows:*
Block the stitchery by pressing it with a damp press cloth and a moderately hot iron.

To assemble a pillow, pin the stitched handkerchief to a second handkerchief (for the backing) with the wrong sides facing. Stitch together about 3 inches from the outside edge of each handkerchief along three sides. (The excess fabric creates a tailored border around each of the pillows.)

Insert a pillow form or stuff firmly with polyester fiberfill; top-stitch the opening closed.

If you use plaid fabrics, ginghams, or any other fabrics that have unfinished edges, hem the edges with a double-rolled hem. Then, assemble as directed above.

*T*his ever-fresh apron is a delight to wear, whether donned for kitchen duty or paired with your wardrobe for a charming fashion accent.

MATERIALS
- 10-inch square of magenta broadcloth (bib inset)
- 10-inch square of 12-count waste canvas
- 1½ yards of print fabric
- ¾ yard of solid fabric (lining)
- Embroidery floss in colors listed under the color key
- Sewing thread to match printed fabric

INSTRUCTIONS
Refer to the sections on pages 18-19, 32-33, and 54-55 for cross-stitching tips and techniques, and for materials that are necessary for working all counted cross-stitch projects.

The inset is 6½ inches square.
- *To prepare the pattern:*
Chart pattern, *right*, onto graph paper using felt-tip marking pens.
- *To prepare the materials:*
See tips, page 42, for working with waste canvas, and prepare magenta fabric for cross-stitching.

Separate the floss and use two strands for working cross-stitches.
- *To stitch the floral inset:*
Stitch the flower design. Outline the petals with backstitches using brown embroidery floss; outline the leaves with green.
- *To assemble the apron:*
Remove canvas and press stitchery.

For bib, trim stitchery to measure 7½ inches square. From print fabric cut lining the same size, and two 2x7½-inch strips for the top bib bands.

Use ¼-inch seams, and assemble pieces with right sides facing.

Place long edge of one top bib band atop top edge of stitchery; sew along edge. Press open. Repeat for lining and remaining top bib band.

Sew stitchery to lining along top edge, turn and press. Topstitch ¼ inch from *lower* edge of band.

For the straps, cut and piece enough fabric to make four 2x60-inch strips (two straps, two facings).

Sew straps to facings, leaving one short edge open and leaving an 8¼-inch opening at bottom for bib insert. Repeat for other strap. Turn; press seam allowances to inside.

Matching raw edges, sew open ends of straps to bib front.

Fold facings toward back and slip-stitch to bib back; topstitch ¼ inch from strap edges.

From print fabric cut two 1x4-inch waistband loops. Fold in half lengthwise, folding raw edges under; topstitch.

For waistband, cut two 2x21½-inch strips. Center bib along one long edge of waistband. Sew waistbands together along this edge.

For loops, fold loops in half; insert into short ends of waistbands. Stitch short ends. Turn and press.

For the skirt, cut a 31-inch-wide apron skirt from border print and solid fabric (lining). Cut skirt to length desired.

Stitch lining to skirt around bottom and side edges. Turn and press. Gather top edge of skirt; stitch to one of the remaining long edges of the waistband. Turn, press, and slip-stitch waistband closed. Topstitch top and ends of waistband.

Criss-cross straps in back. Tuck straps into loops and tie.

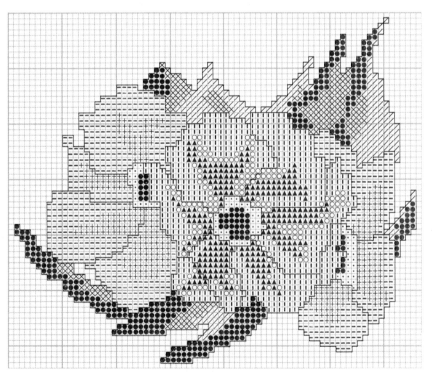

1 Square = 1 Stitch

COLOR KEY

◉	**Dark Green**	◌	**Medium Pink**
⊠	**Medium Green**	Ⅱ	**Light Pink**
⧄	**Light Green**	⊞	**Medium Lavender**
▲	**Dark Pink**	⊟	**Light Lavender**
		·	**Brown**

*S*pecial occasions are remembered forever with handmade stitchery mementos.

The pillow, opposite, combines cross-stitch with cutwork for an exquisite ring bearer's pillow. Or, stitch a name and date in the pillow center to commemorate a birth, anniversary, or graduation.

The same floral motifs are stitched into a picture frame to border a favorite photograph.

Ring Bearer's Pillow

The pillow is 13x13 inches.

——————— MATERIALS ———————
· 14-inch square of ecru hardanger
· ½ yard of blue fabric (lining, backing, ruffle)
· 1¼ yards of 1½-inch-wide ecru lace
· Embroidery floss in colors listed under the color key
· Polyester fiberfill
· 1 yard *each* of ¹⁄₁₆-inch-wide light and dark blue ribbons

——————— INSTRUCTIONS ———————
• *To prepare the pattern:*
Chart the *larger* motif on the diagram, *at right*, into the corner of a large sheet of graph paper using felt-tip marking pens.

Note: The smaller motif is for the mirror frame.

Chart same pattern onto a second sheet of graph paper; cut out.

On the large sheet of graph paper, position the cutout pattern so it is directly opposite the original charted pattern. (Draw a diagonal line on the graph paper for a guide.) Draw a square around the charted

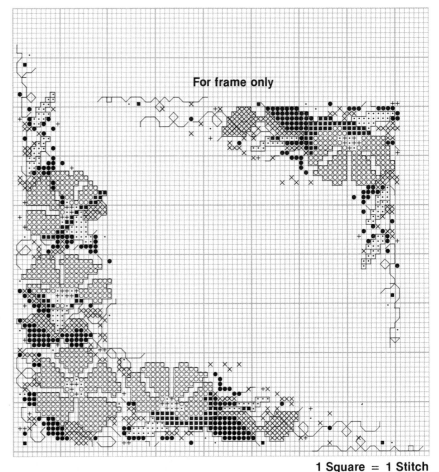

For frame only

1 Square = 1 Stitch

COLOR KEY

■ Royal Blue	● Evergreen	⊞ Peach
◲ Light Blue	⊠ Light Green	⊡ Yellow

pattern eight squares outside the edge of the design.
• *To stitch the pillow:*
Use two strands of floss to work stitches over two threads of fabric.

Stitch tendrils on the design using dark green embroidery floss.

Outline the flowers using contrasting colors of floss.
Stitch a cutwork design in the center area if desired. (Refer to books on the topic for patterns.)
• *To assemble the pillow:*
Trim pillow to size, adding ½ inch for seam allowances. Cut lining and backing the same size.

Cut a 4-inch-wide length from blue fabric for ruffle, adding ½-inch seam allowance. Fold in half lengthwise; gather. Stitch lace to ruffle. Baste lining to wrong side of pillow top. Sew ruffle to pillow top.

With right sides facing, stitch top to back, leaving an opening for turning. Turn, press, stuff, and stitch opening closed.

Cut ribbon in half; fold in half again. Stitch two ribbons to opposite pillow corners. Slip rings on ribbons; tie ribbons in bows.

Floral Picture Frame

The frame is 13x15 inches.

MATERIALS
- 17x19 inches *each* of yellow hardanger, lining fabric, quilt batting, and heavy cardboard
- Embroidery floss

INSTRUCTIONS
- *To prepare the pattern:*
Rule graph paper off in increments of eight squares to the inch.

Determine measurement of photograph opening. (Each inch equals eight squares on the graph paper.) Chart opening onto graph paper.

Chart large motif, *opposite*, to corner of graph paper. Chart small motif, *opposite*, to opposite corner.
- *To stitch the piece:*
Use three floss strands to work stitches over three fabric threads.

Stitch tendrils with dark green floss. Outline flowers with contrasting floss colors.
- *To assemble the piece:*
Cut opening for photo, adding ½ inch for seam allowances; cut batting and lining the same size.

Baste batting to wrong side of stitchery. Sew front to lining, right sides facing, along photograph opening. Clip corners, trim, turn, and press. Glue picture to cardboard. Stretch stitchery over cardboard; frame (see tips, page 53).

A gift of bed linens is especially cherished when personalized with touches of cross-stitched embroidery.

A spritely border of butter-cups trims the purchased sheet and pillowcases at right. The same motif is stitched onto a tiny square, and then pieced, log-cabin style, into a bright patchwork pillow.

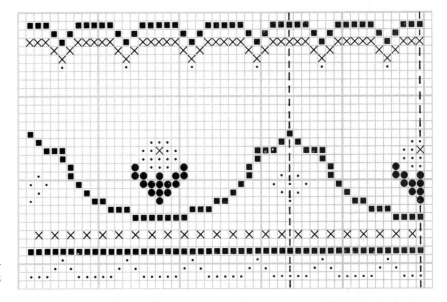

Pillowcases and Sheet

MATERIALS

- Purchased pillowcases and sheet
- Light blue, dark blue, yellow, and green embroidery floss
- 10-count waste canvas to cover stitched areas

INSTRUCTIONS

• *To prepare patterns:*
Chart diagram, *above right,* onto graph paper using felt-tip marking pens. To complete the pattern, flop the area between the *dashed* lines to the desired length. *Note:* Eliminate the top two scalloped rows for the pillowcase design.

• *To prepare the materials:*
Remove hem on pillowcases and top edge of sheet.

• *To stitch pillowcases and sheet:*
Use three strands of floss for working cross-stitches.

Baste length of waste canvas to *right* side of top edge of sheet and pillowcase bands. Be sure to center a *square* of waste canvas in the center of the width of the sheet and the pillowcase bands.

Note: Do not piece canvas, since resulting stitches will be uneven and misshapen.

Pull needle through the *tiniest* holes on the waste canvas. Be careful not to catch the waste canvas as you stitch; otherwise, removing the canvas threads becomes difficult.

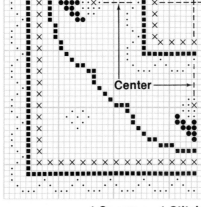

Center

1 Square = 1 Stitch

COLOR KEY

■ Dark Blue	◉ Green
⊠ Light Blue	⊡ Yellow

Work the border design on the sheet so the flowers are right side up when the bed is made. (When sheet is hemmed, the flowers will be upside down; however, design appears right side up when the top edge is folded back.) Work the pillowcase design so the scalloped edges face open edge of pillowcase.

Begin stitching with the *center* of the design in the center of the width of the sheet and pillowcases; work the design outward to the edges.

• *To finish:*
Moisten the waste canvas and pull out the threads.

Press the stitcheries and re-hem sheet and pillowcases.

Monogrammed Log-Cabin Pillow

The pillow is approximately 12x12 inches.

MATERIALS

- 8x8 inches of white 14-count Aida cloth
- ½ yard of backing fabric
- Embroidery floss in colors listed under the color key
- 3 shades of blue print fabric
- 1½ yards of yellow piping
- No. 5 yellow pearl cotton floss
- Polyester fiberfill or a purchased pillow form

INSTRUCTIONS

• *To prepare the pattern:*
Chart diagram, *opposite below,* onto graph paper using felt-tip marking pens. This is one-quarter of the pattern. Flop the diagram once to make half of the pattern. Flop it once again to complete the pattern.

Chart an initial in the center of the stitchery if desired (see pages 16-17 for an alphabet design).

• *To stitch the pillow:*
Use two strands of embroidery floss for working cross-stitches over one space of the Aida cloth.

• *To assemble the pillow:*
Trim fabric ½ inch from the edge of the stitchery. Cut four 2½-inch-wide strips from *each* of the print fabrics. (Measurements include ½ inch for seam allowances.)

Sew the strips to the stitchery in a log-cabin fashion. Quilt ¼ inch from all seam lines using yellow pearl cotton floss.

Sew yellow piping to pillow top.

With right sides facing, stitch the pillow top to the backing, leaving an opening for turning. Turn pillow to the right side, stuff with polyester fiberfill (or a pillow form), and stitch the opening closed.

Festive Christmas Stitchery

A season of warmth and hospitality, Christmas is a perfect time to display your most festive handcrafted treasures. To help you celebrate in style, here are designs and crafts to cross-stitch, including a sampler and greeting cards, an elegant tablecloth, table runner and napkins, an afghan, and tabletop decorations, too.

With its traditional holiday blessing, the sampler, *opposite,* extends a cheerful welcome to family and guests. And what nicer way to convey your best wishes to loved ones than with greeting cards embellished with a wreath, tree, or other symbols of the season.

For how-to instructions and patterns, please turn the page.

Cross-Stitched Greeting Cards

————— MATERIALS —————
- 18-count white Davosa fabric (or a suitable substitute)
- Red, light and dark geen, yellow, and brown embroidery floss
- White or colored card stock papers and matching envelopes
- White glue
- Colored graphic art tape
- Mat knife
- Transparent tape

————— INSTRUCTIONS —————
• *To prepare the patterns:*
Chart patterns, *below,* onto graph paper using felt-tip marking pens.

Create the mirror image of *each* diagram by flopping the motifs to complete the patterns.

• *To prepare the materials:*
Separate the embroidery floss and use two strands for working cross-stitches over two threads of fabric.

• *To stitch the cards:*
Stitch the designs leaving approximately two inches of unworked fabric around each of the designs. Trim away any excess fabric.

Press stitcheries with a damp pressing cloth and a moderately hot iron.

• *Assembling the cards:*
Determine the size of the finished note card to frame your stitchery. Draw these measurements onto the wrong side of white or colored paper; cut out.

Determine the size of the opening for the stitchery insert. Draw the measurements onto the wrong side of the front flap.

Cut out the opening, using a mat knife.

Glue or tape each stitchery to the back of the card fronts.

Border the stitchery on the front side of each greeting card with narrow bands of graphic art tape for a colorful finish.

Buy or make matching envelopes.

Festive Holiday Sampler

The sampler, shown on page 66, measures 14¼x18½ inches.

————— MATERIALS —————
- 16x20-inch piece of white 18-count Davosa fabric (or suitable substitute)
- 2 skeins *each* of light green, medium green, and red embroidery floss
- 1 skein *each* of yellow, brown, dark brown, and gray embroidery floss

————— INSTRUCTIONS —————
See pages 18-19, 32-33, and 54-55 for special cross-stitching tips and techniques, and for materials necessary for working cross-stitch projects.

• *To prepare the pattern:*
Chart the diagram, *opposite,* onto graph paper.

• *To stitch the sampler:*
Use three strands of floss and work stitches over two threads of fabric.

Locate center of pattern and center of fabric; begin stitching here. Or, begin stitching in one corner of the border pattern of tiny houses.

Note: Be sure to allow extra fabric around the sampler for framing.

• *To finish the sampler:*
Press the finished piece to block it.

Frame the sampler as desired. (See tips, page 53, for specific framing instructions.)

TIPS

How To Prevent Dye Stains

Laundering a piece of embroidery is virtually foolproof, provided you have properly prepared all of the materials and have checked them for colorfastness.

However, if you are washing a treasured piece of embroidery and discover that the fabric or thread colors begin to bleed, it is most important that you do not panic.

The suggestions that follow will help prevent (or at least minimize) stains, should you find yourself in just such a predicament.

The first rule is to keep the stitchery under the water. Run water over the piece until all of the dye is completely flushed out and the water is crystal clear.

Then, roll the piece in a clean towel; squeeze out excess moisture. Continue to roll stitchery in additional towels, and squeeze, until the piece is as moisture-free as possible.

Lay the embroidery out flat to dry. Use rustproof pins to pin the piece in place on a surface of clean plywood or foam core board.

Allow embroidery to dry thoroughly. Remove pins, then press stitchery carefully using a damp press cloth and a warm iron.

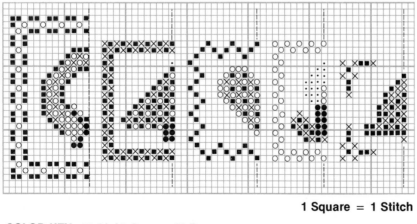

1 Square = 1 Stitch

COLOR KEY ⊠ **Light Green** ⬤ **Brown**
⊡ **Red** ■ **Evergreen** ⬚ **Yellow**

CHRISTMAS 1984

Peace Be In This House

abcdefghijkl
mnopqrstuvwxyz
1234567890

COLOR KEY   ◪ Brown   ◼ Dark Green   ◎ Light Green

◉ Medium Green   ⊠ Red   ⊡ Yellow

1 Square = 1 Stitch

*W*hen your family and closest friends gather together for Christmas feasting, set them down to a festive table bedecked with the holiday linen, opposite. The tablecloth is made of an elegant fabric—designed especially for counted embroidery—and is cross-stitched with holiday motifs. You can use the motifs in lots of other ways, too. For suggestions, see below.

MATERIALS

- 43x57-inch piece of Zweigart® Alba fabric (available through Art Needlework Treasure Trove, Box 2440, Grand Central Station, New York, NY 10163)
- No. 5 pearl cotton floss in colors listed under the color key

INSTRUCTIONS

Refer to pages 18-19, 32-33, and 54-55 for special cross-stitching tips and techniques, and for materials that are necessary for working all counted cross-stitch projects.

- *To prepare the patterns:*
Chart diagrams, *right,* onto graph paper using felt-tip marking pens. Make a mirror image by flopping the symbols to complete patterns.

- *To stitch the tablecloth:*
Work each stitch over one thread of fabric using pearl cotton floss.

Find the center point of each fabric square to begin stitching.

Alternately stitch a wreath and tree in each square.

Continue alternating the motifs to fill the length and width of the tablecloth. Trim the woven borders

with single holly motifs, if desired (see photograph, *opposite*).

- *To finish the tablecloth:*
Hem the raw edges of the tablecloth or border the edges with a decorative trim.

- *Creative ways with patterns:*
Instead of making a Christmas tablecloth, cross-stitch wreath and tree motifs down the center of a fabric strip to make a table runner.

Work designs over one thread of hardanger for festive coasters.

Use the tree and wreath motifs, minus the holly borders, and work them over one thread of fabric for delicate ornaments. Cut out the shapes and sew to a fabric backing,

leaving an opening for turning. Stuff with fiberfill and stitch the opening closed. Attach ribbon loop for hanging. Sew colored beads and pearls onto ornaments for highlights, if desired.

You can use the motifs to stitch up a Christmas coverlet, too. Work each design on hardanger fabric; alternate a cross-stitched square with a plain fabric square. Sew squares together; bind with sashing strips, and quilt with Christmas motifs or other traditional quilting patterns.

With just a little imagination, it's easy to create pillows, sweet-scented sachets, box-top covers, and all kinds of other Christmas ideas.

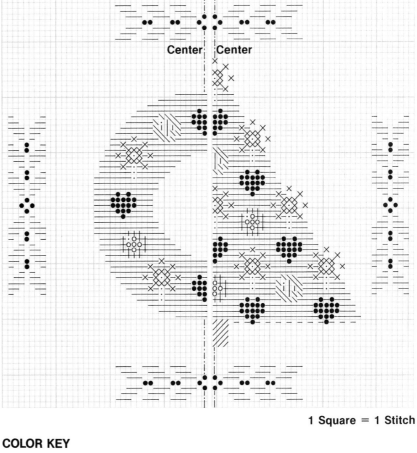

1 Square = 1 Stitch

COLOR KEY

⊟ Green	⊞ Purple	⧄ Brown
⬤ Red	⧄ Blue	① Light Blue
⊠ Yellow	⊡ Gray	⧄ Light Purple

HOLIDAY SLEIGH

*C*hildren love Christmas, and spend many an eager hour awaiting the arrival of Saint Nicholas.

Just imagine the excitement Christmas morning when they find Santa's gifts tucked inside the cornucopia ornaments and miniature sleigh, opposite!

Use the cornucopias and sleigh for party favors and a table centerpiece, too, and fill each with candy and small treasures for your guests to take home.

Both are crafted from sheets of perforated paper and trimmed with cross-stitched holly and poinsettia motifs. To decorate the ornaments use the smaller designs from the sleigh and stitch them at random on quarter-circle shapes.

MATERIALS

For the sleigh:
- Two 12x18-inch sheets of ecru (or white) perforated paper (available through Astor Place, Ltd., 239 Main Avenue, Stirling, NJ 07980)
- Four (40-m) spools of DMC gold metallic embroidery floss
- Embroidery floss in the following colors: light and dark red, light and dark green, yellow, brown, and black
- Bristol board
- Heavy-bodied white glue, such as Tacky glue
- Narrow gold braid and red and green ribbons (trims)
- Water-erasable marking pens

For the cornucopias:
- Sheets of perforated paper
- Embroidery floss in the colors listed above
- Tacky glue
- Narrow lace, gold braid, and red or green ribbons (trims)

INSTRUCTIONS

• *To prepare the patterns:*

For the sleigh sides, transfer the sleigh diagram, on page 74, onto graph paper using felt-tip marking pens. Do not add seam allowances.

Create the opposite side of the sleigh by flopping the diagram, and making a mirror image.

Note: The easiest and most accurate way to do this (and produce identical sides on the sleigh) is to carefully cut out the diagram above. Place diagram, *facedown*, against a sheet of graph paper, carefully aligning the squares.

Trace the outline onto the graph paper; remove the original pattern.

Chart motifs onto pattern, flopping them if desired.

Or, you may wish to transfer only one sleigh side and one runner to start. Stitch them up, and cut them out. Then place them facedown atop a sheet of perforated paper and trace the outlines onto the perforated paper, using the same method as described above for creating graph-paper patterns.

For the runners, repeat procedure, as directed above for sleigh sides, to chart runners, page 75.

For the center panel, cut out a 3½x14¼-inch rectangle from perforated paper. Draw a line across the width (on the wrong side of the paper) 25 squares down from one short edge. This line is a fold line. Set the panel aside.

• *To stitch the sleigh:*

Use two strands of metallic floss and two strands of embroidery floss for working cross-stitches over one space of the perforated paper.

For the sleigh body, stitch the poinsettia and holly motifs onto both sides of the sleigh. Outline the poinsettia petals with one strand of brown embroidery floss.

For the runners, work cross-stitches using gold floss; outline the shapes as indicated on diagram using one strand of black floss.

For the center panel, stitch the double holly motif (shown in the middle of the sleigh side pattern) centered in the 25-square area.

Stitch a small poinsettia just beneath the holly motif. This is the *front* end of the center panel.

At the opposite end, stitch a poinsettia motif. Add more motifs to the center panel, if desired. Fold the panel along the marked line so the right sides face each other.

• *To assemble the sleigh:*

Cut out sleigh sides and runners.

Trace the side shapes onto white bristol board; cut out.

Trace the outline of the center panel onto bristol board, adding ½-inch margins to the two long sides. Mark fold line on center panel onto bristol board; fold.

continued

72

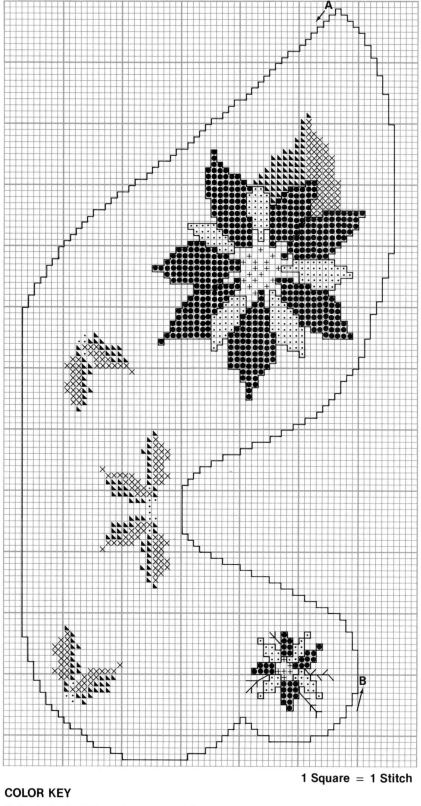

Cut out along margin line in a sawtooth manner (it should resemble pinking shears). This sawtoothed edge makes it possible to glue the panel to the curved edges of the sleigh body.

To assemble bristol-board pieces, glue the center panel to the body sections, placing area above the folded line (on the center panel) around the curved area in the front of the sleigh. *Note:* Place the sawtooth margins on the *outside* of the side sections to give the inside of the sleigh a finished look.

Place glue on the wrong side of all stitched areas of perforated paper shapes, and then all around the outer edges. (Use glue sparingly so it does not seep through the perforations.) Place the perforated paper shapes atop bristol board shapes; allow glue to dry thoroughly.

Glue gold braid trim around all of the edges to cover seam joints and trim the raw edges at the top of the sleigh.

Glue the tabs of the runners to the bottom of the sleigh.

Note: A narrow brace may be required between the runners to keep them from spreading apart.

Trim the sleigh with red and green ribbon bows, if desired.

For cornucopias, draw a quarter circle with a 4¼-inch radius onto perforated paper; add a ½-inch tab to one straight side, tapering one edge of the tab to a point.

Stitch random holly or poinsettia motifs onto the perforated paper following instructions above.

Place glue on tab; fold paper into cone shape, with the tapered end of the tab forming the point of the cone. Glue tab to inside of cone; allow glue to dry thoroughly.

Trim the top of the cornucopia with lace and gold braid trims. Add red and green ribbon bows, and a loop for hanging. Fill with candy and small trinkets, if desired.

1 Square = 1 Stitch

COLOR KEY

● Dark Red	◩ Dark Green	⊞ Yellow
⊡ Red	⊠ Green	■ Gold Metallic

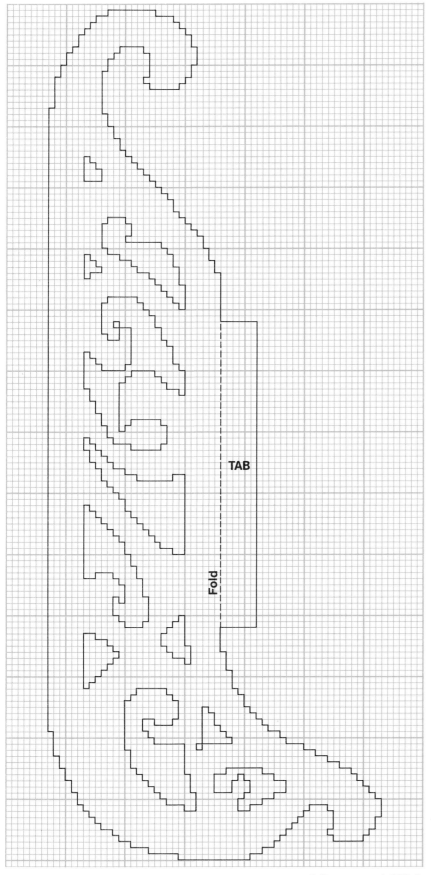

TAB

Fold

1 Square = 1 Stitch

Creating Designs

Even if designing isn't your forté, you can still create pretty stitchery with a personal touch by collecting cross-stitch motifs and then arranging them until you achieve a pleasing design. The tips below will help you design cross-stitch originals to make for yourself, your family, and friends. And each gift of stitchery is a cherished treasure because it's a one-of-a-kind design.

Collecting patterns: Begin by browsing through current crafts books and magazines. Keep an eye out for needlepoint, filet crochet, and fair isle knitting patterns, too, since these patterns translate easily into cross-stitch designs.

Clip designs that are appealing, or copy patterns onto graph paper. (If you want to take creative license, this is the time to change motif shapes and colors.) Search for old pattern books and stitcheries at antique shops and garage sales, too. Or, look through coloring and other children's books for design possibilities. (Lay picture atop a light box, place graph paper over the picture, and chart with crosses.)

Organizing designs: Place patterns between acetate sheets for protection; assemble in ring binder.

For your convenience, divide patterns into sections labeled by subject matter—alphabets, Christmas motifs, animals, flowers, etc.

Creating original designs: As special occasions approach, pull out the booklet and select motifs that are appropriate. If a name or message is included, chart this first; then arrange additional motifs.

It's easiest to design patterns with a repeat motif. For a pillow, start with a quarter of the total design; complete it by making mirror images. Create a picture similarly, except design half of the project and flop it to complete the image. To make a sampler, chart out alphabet, message, and name, then combine with border patterns.

Christmas warmth and elegance are easy to create with the table runner and matching napkins shown here.

A black background sets off the richness of the green, gold, and bits of red in this design. (Against white fabric, the motifs look entirely different.)

The borders are fringed and hemstitched with lustrous gold metallic threads.

———— MATERIALS ————
- 18-inch-wide piece of black hardanger in a length suitable for your table (for runner only)
- 15-inch squares of black hardanger (for napkins only)
- Green, light green, red, and gold embroidery floss
- Gold metallic embroidery floss

———— INSTRUCTIONS ————
See pages 18-19, 32-33, and 54-55 for special cross-stitch tips and techniques, and for materials that are necessary for working all counted cross-stitch projects.

The table runner is 16x88 inches. Napkins measure 13x13-inches.
- *To prepare the patterns:*

For runner, the arrow on the diagram, *right,* marks the center of the *width* of the design. One complete motif is shown. Portions of repeat motifs are shown to indicate placement of others.

Transfer the diagram onto graph paper using felt-tip marking pens.

Note: It is unnecessary to chart out the entire table runner design, although it may be helpful.

The runner should begin and end with complete holly motifs.

Charting out the entire design will help determine the length of black hardanger to purchase. (Allow 5 inches of fabric on each end of the runner for a plain border.)

For napkins, transfer the diagram, *below,* onto graph paper using felt-tip marking pens, if desired.
- *To stitch the runner and napkins:*

For runner, use three strands of embroidery floss and two strands of metallic embroidery floss to work

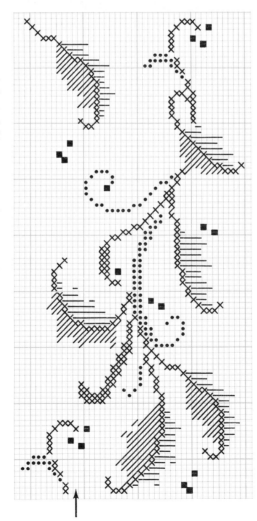

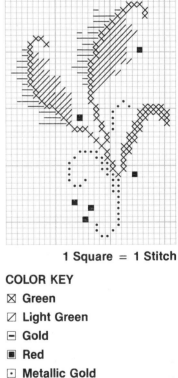

1 Square = 1 Stitch

COLOR KEY
⊠ **Green**
⊘ **Light Green**
⊟ **Gold**
◼ **Red**
⊡ **Metallic Gold**

the cross-stitches. Work each cross-stitch over *three* threads of hardanger fabric.

Locate both the center of design width (see arrow on diagram) and fabric width at one end; mark the fabric center with a pin. Move pin 5 inches from edge of fabric. Begin stitching at this point.

Finish stitching the runner with a complete motif, allowing 5 inches of fabric for the border at the opposite end.

For napkins, use two strands of floss and one strand of metallic thread for working cross-stitches over *two* threads of fabric. Work motif 3 inches from corner edges.

• *To finish the runner and napkins:*
For runner, measure and mark, with a straight pin, 3 inches from the outermost points of the stitchery on all sides. Pull four threads along pins on *all* sides.

Hemstitch using two strands of metallic thread. (See tips, on page 58, for hemstitching instructions.)

Trim fabric along a thread of hardanger 1 inch from hemstitching. Pull threads to fringe.

For napkins, measure 1 inch from outermost stitches on two adjacent sides of the stitched design; mark with pins. From the pins, measure 12 inches; mark with pins. Pull threads, hemstitch, and fringe as directed above for runner.

A *toasty fire and this cozy coverlet, opposite, are the perfect team to ward off winter's chilliest nights.*

The coverlet is made from a unique fabric designed especially for working counted cross-stitch embroidery. Squares of red and green are stitched in the center of the open even-weave areas and bordered by bands of prewoven pattern.

Fill decorative squares with letters, hearts, or other favorite motifs of your own choosing.

─────MATERIALS─────
- 1¼ yards of Zweigart's Novara® ivory embroidery fabric (available through Hansi House, 246 5th Ave., New York, NY 10001)
- Green, pink, and red No. 3 pearl cotton floss
- 5½ yards of 1½-inch-wide red velvet ribbon
- Commercial cross-stitch alphabet charts

─────INSTRUCTIONS─────
Refer to the special sections on pages 18-19, 32-33, and 54-55 for cross-stitching tips and techniques, and for materials that are necessary for working cross-stitch projects.

The finished size of the coverlet is 43x50½ inches. It is five blocks wide and six blocks deep.
- *To prepare the pattern:*
Transfer the pattern, *at right,* onto graph paper using felt-tip marking pens. Flop the pattern to complete the design. *Note:* This is the pattern for the corner blocks.

For the remaining blocks, place a letter of the alphabet in the center of each wreath motif. (From a commercial leaflet, select an alphabet that fits inside the wreath of each square.) Alternate the embroidery colors for the alphabet blocks, making some of the borders green (instead of red) and some of the wreaths red (instead of green).

Chart letters inside the center of each wreath, if desired, using a green felt-tip marking pen. Make any necessary adjustments to the alphabet at this time.
- *To stitch the coverlet:*
Stitch cross-stitches with pearl cotton floss. Work each cross-stitch over one thread of fabric.

Locate the center of a square and the center of the pattern and begin stitching at this point. Work outward from the center point.
- *Finishing the coverlet:*
Press the stitchery on the wrong side using a damp press cloth and a moderately hot iron.

Trim coverlet yardage ¾ inch beyond the outer edge of outside fabric border.

Fold velvet ribbon in half lengthwise and machine-stitch to coverlet to hide raw edges.

A note on specialty fabrics: Although even-weave fabrics such as Aida cloth and hardanger are the usual choices for working counted cross-stitch designs, a variety of other decorative cross-stitch fabrics are on the market and make wonderful alternatives to the more traditional selections.

These fabrics are enhanced with simple, but elegant design motifs and with open areas of even-weave fabric that allow for cross-stitch embellishment.

Zweigart® Fabrics, from Germany, carries a beautiful, high-quality line of these specialty fabrics. The designs range from checkerboard, diamond, and leaf patterns to rich floral damask patterns with rosebud and tulip motifs. Each has open areas for working counted-thread stitchery motifs.

These novelty fabrics are enormously versatile. They are suitable for making tablecloths, runners, bellpulls, book covers, afghans, pillows, and garments.

The fabrics come in three colors—eggshell, white, and cream. They are 100 percent polyacrylics and cotton/rayon blends, so they all are easy to care for.

While many of the fabrics are machine-washable, it is probably best to launder them by hand using a mild laundry soap. If you should decide to wash them in a machine, set the machine on a cold-water, gentle cycle. Then, lay the piece out flat to dry.

1 Square = 1 Stitch

COLOR KEY
× Red
╱ Green
• Pink

79

ACKNOWLEDGMENTS

We extend our sincere thanks and appreciation to each of the following talented people who contributed designs and projects to this book.

Pauline Asmus—73
Dixie Falls—30, 56
Margie Gill—66
Diane Hayes—4, 59, 63,
Laura Holtorf—4-11, 20, 38, 41-42, 44, 46, 48, 50-51, 56, 59, 63, 65, 76-77
Ann Levine—20-21, 24, 26, 65, 70, 76-78
Polly D. McCarthy—60
Susan Veigulis—42
Jim Williams—46

We are also happy to acknowledge the following photographers, whose creative talents and technical skills contributed much to this book.

Mike Dieter—Cover, 18-19, 32-33, 54-55
Hedrich-Blessing—24, 40, 51
Thomas Hooper—34-36, 76-77
Hopkins Associates—26, 38, 46, 48, 59
Scott Little—4-11, 20-21, 42, 44-45, 50, 56-57, 63, 65, 73
Perry Struse—30, 60, 66-67, 70, 78

For their creative skills, courtesy, and cooperation, we extend a special thanks to:

Pauline Asmus, Pearl Beal, Barbara Bergman, Gary Boling, Pat Byer, Jo Downey, Donna Glas, Mary Lou Griffith, Diane Hayes, Dorothy Hohnbaum, Sara Donna Jensen, Lois Lloyd, Julie O'Brien, Pam Onken,

Diane Pratt, Margaret Sindelar, Susan Veigulis, Julie Wiemann, Judy Williamson

Astor Place, Ltd.
  239 Main Ave.
  Stirling, NJ 07980
C. M. Offray & Son, Inc.
  261 Madison Ave.
  New York, NY 10016
DMC
  107 Trumbull St.
  Elizabeth, NJ 07206
Joan Toggit Ltd.
  246 Fifth Ave.
  New York, NY 10001

Pella Historical Society
  Pella, Iowa
Woodlawn Plantation
  Mount Vernon, Virginia